DUDLEY SPARKS
AND THE EIGHTH
INVITATION

Dudley Sparks and the Eighth Invitation

A Catholic Kidz Book Series #1

Dorothy Turner-Jones

Mom—
Dad—

I love you!

To all of the children
Wherever you are...
God loves you!
You have not been forgotten.

CONTENTS

CHAPTER 1

ALL ABOUT ME!

I t's already 11:00 a.m., and I've been standing out here forever! I'm waiting for Mr. Stevens. Where is he, anyway? Hummm... hold on!

Could it be? I think I see someone coming... yes! Mr. Stevens just turned the corner onto my block. I'd recognize that slow, steady stride anywhere!

Oh, excuse me. I guess you're wondering who Mr. Stevens is. Mr. Stevens is our mail carrier and my friend. And, well, I guess you are also wondering who I am. Please allow me to introduce myself. I am Vincent Lexington Jones, or VJ for short. I am in the fifth grade at St. Lawrence O'Toole School in Quincy, Illinois. For the most part, I'm just a regular kid. In fact, most people would say that I'm a pretty nice guy. Adults tell me all the time how special I am.

And I'm sure people tell you the same thing too. But just in case you forget—or in case people forget to tell you—you are special!

My mom says that all kids are unique and that God sprinkles special talents and gifts onto all of His children, and she's right. Yep! We all are special! At first, it was hard figuring out just what gifts God gave me. I play tennis, but I am really not that good. Most times, I hit my knee with the racquet instead of hitting the ball. I play the piano, but I'm still on "Twinkle, Twinkle, Little Star" after seven years of lessons. Ms. Diane, my piano teacher, says I don't practice enough. But, like Mom says, God gives us all something great. You see, I am a really big kid. Well, not big, but really, really, tall.

God showered, not sprinkled, me with the gift of height! Being tall is great. But it can also be detrimental and even hazardous to your health!

Since preschool, I've always been last in line on picture day—and I mean always! "Vincent, honey, you're at the back," teachers would politely say. So, like clockwork, year after year, teachers would quietly escort me to the end of every picture-day line. By fourth grade, I had it figured out. Big boy, straight to the back! Going to the Saturday matinee can be tricky for tall kids, too. Most times, I slide down in my chair. It's no fun listening to kids complain that they can't see because of the tall man in front of them (meaning me)!

The junior high kids don't give me a break either. For example, last Sunday on my way to receive Communion, I heard two eighth graders say, "Look at the feet on that fifth grader!" They laughed so loud that Father Francis gave them a long frown. The list of complaints about being tall can go on until eternity—infinity even!

Listed are a few more examples:

I'm too tall for my bunk bed. My feet hang over the edge when I'm lying down. At night, I feel like all of my blood is rushing to my toes. Clothes, of course, are an issue! The one-size-fits-all doesn't fit. They are either too long, too short, too wide, or too narrow! I feel like the world is a size medium, and I'm an extra-large.

Now, don't get me wrong—being tall is kind of cool. You can call me a portable step stool. Stacking books, shelving supplies, and decorating the classroom has been my job since first grade. I also remove small objects from the top of my classmates' heads. You would not believe some of the things that I've found! Examples below:

Earrings, combs, cookie crumbs, pencil shavings—I've seen it all!

Being tall definitely has its benefits, just like being short has its benefits too! But stretching out at once has been challenging, and even downright frustrating! My body just doesn't know where to go. So it goes all over the place. To say the least, I'm clumsy. I stumble, slide, and slip everywhere—and I do mean everywhere! When I was younger, I fell every day. I just couldn't get that walking thing right. Of course, most times my mom scooped me up when I tripped. She was quick. But now, I'm almost twice her size and weight. So when my feet forget what to do, I either tumble to the ground or find a way to balance my body all by myself. Which usually means that I fall!

Unfortunately, injuries and damage to property go hand in hand. I stagger on escalators, topple over carts in grocery stores, and demolish small animal habitats on educational field trips. My legs and feet seem to have a mind of their own. I bump and bang my toes up the steps. I bruise, scratch, and scrape my knees going down the steps. But other parts of my body work just fine. For example, my face is doing better. Some of my acne is finally clearing up. There are actually sections on my face where there are no pimples at all!

My brain is not that bad either. I'm pretty smart. I usually get A grades in reading, religion, gym, and science. Math and social studies grades wobble between Bs and C+s.

Physical education is my favorite subject, but my mom told me to change my favorite subject to reading or science— I'd sound more intellectual! My eyesight, however, is marginal at best. I have two permanent eyes and two temporary eyes, thanks to Benjamin Franklin. He invented bifocals, you know. Oh yeah, I can't forget about my pearly white teeth! I could actually do toothpaste commercials for a living.

But the thing that makes me really special is my heart. It is in the best shape of all! I am a happy kid most of the time. I love my school, my church, and my family. In fact, I have a pretty good life. I have an older brother, Justin. He lives at college in Brownsville, Tennessee. Justin wants to play in a band, live in a log cabin, and get lots of tattoos. But Dad wants Justin to wear a suit and work behind a big desk surrounded by lots of dusty books. They argue!

Andrew, or Drew for short, is my younger brother. He lives at home with me! Andrew is in all-day preschool at Saint Lawrence O'Toole. I wish there was a Saturday and Sunday preschool too. Sometimes my younger brother can be a pest. Anyway, Andrew loves his pet Betta fish, James, and his stuffed animals. But he absolutely, positively hates to turn off the lights at bedtime. This creates havoc in the Jones household, to say the least. Drew cannot sleep without lots of light. At times, the room is so bright that I toss and turn until the alarm sounds the next day. And while Drew may be afraid of the dark, he is fierce on the basketball court! And he really loves the Chicago Bulls basketball team. So it only makes sense that his stuffed animal, Benny the Bull, is his official best friend.

Speaking of friends ... having friends—or even one friend—is cool. A friend can be a grandparent, a neighbor, or a sibling. I have five friends: Nelson, Reed, Zander, Alex, and Walker. You could say that we are brothers, too. We have known each other for a long time. They are great with a capital G!

Speaking of greatness ... it is a super great day for two great reasons! First, today is my birthday: October 17, the day I was born eleven years ago at Saint James Hospital. Today is also the day that I should get my invitation to my very first sleepover. Me, Vincent Lexington Jones, the birthday boy—going to a sleepover! It's almost official because Mr. Stevens is definitely, absolutely, positively here!

CHAPTER 2

A PROMISE IS A PROMISE...RIGHT?

G ood morning, Mr. Stevens!" I drool and dribble with endless anticipation. "What ya got in that bag for me?"

"Well, good morning, Vincent. No school today, huh?"

I respond quickly, "Not today, Mr. Stevens." My eyes focus on his idle hands. "Today is a free day. The teachers have meetings or something," I mumble politely. I've learned that the more I talk, the less Mr. Stevens delivers the mail. And I really want him to keep working.

"Isn't it a beautiful day for walking?" Mr. Steven's asks.

"Beautiful, yes, beautiful," I utter, with a quick smile, still eyeballing that mailbag. I nod twice. Quickly, my eyes travel back to the mailbag because the only thing that I am interested in at this moment is the mail. I am not interested in the birds nor the morning breeze. Not even the sun and the trees, I mumble. The mail! I'm interested in the mail! But—of course—Mr. Stevens rattles on and on!

"Have you been standing out here waiting a long time?" Mr. Stevens asks in his usual courteous manner.

"Yes, but that's OK," I reply. Hey, I think Mr. Stevens is moving his hand. My eyes bounce ... nope.

"I've got all day," he puffs, looking at his pocket watch.

To say the least, I am speechless. And my feet are cold.

"Well," Mr. Stevens announces, patting me lightly on the shoulder, "let me see what I have here in my magic bag. No more dillydallying for me. I've got to get to work."

Finally! Like a high-speed machine, Mr. Stevens shifts into gear. Envelopes, periodicals, newspapers, and postcards fly here and there in search of the mail for 712 East Norris Drive. "Here you go!" Mr. Stevens says, handing me a hefty pile of mail. I try to smile like an eleven-year old ... but I can't hold back the ten-year old smile. It sneaks out all over my face.

"Thanks, Mr. Stevens," I shout, grabbing my bundle like a frenzied bank robber on the lam. Before I can say, "Have a great day," Mr. Stevens was already next door, sharing his gregarious grin and long-winded conversation with the next door neighbors. I immediately tear into the bundle of mail.

"Let's see," I mumble, flipping the mail back and forth. My eager eyes quickly skim and scan the envelopes. "Hum ... let's see," I say quietly, "a bill from the water company? Nope. Interested in a health club membership? Well ...," I mumble to myself, "Dad could stand to lose a pound or two. But nope.

"Yikes! An advertisement for summer school!" I pause. Maybe I should hide this. Better not ...

"A furniture sale? Nope. But those grapes for seventy-nine cents a pound look delicious," I jokily admit to myself.

I rumble through the heap of mail. "But I only have a few more left," I grumble as my eyes carefully dance on the remaining envelopes.

A letter from an insurance company? Boring. And…YES! It's here! It's finally here! The invitation to a Reed Conti sleepover is in my possession—and just in time. I'm hungry and cold. Quickly, I stuff the precious invitation into my pajama pants pocket. The smell of scorched country bacon and overcooked eggs greet me at the front door.

"Did you get the mail, Vincent?" Mom shouts from the smoky kitchen.

"I've got it; be right there," I say.

Just for future reference, my mom isn't a very good cook. She can make breakfast—you know, basic things: eggs, grits, bacon, pancakes—but unfortunately, she makes them over and over and over! She burns them over and over too.

Having a mom who doesn't cook fancy meals is not that bad. I can eat burgers, foot-longs, fries, and apple pie all day, every day. I am a little concerned— like our First Lady, Michelle Obama— about the harmful effects of junk food. But I am even more concerned about my mom burning down the house.

Food is important. Don't get me wrong. But poor cooking is the least of my mom's struggles. Her small body is stuffed with faults that are just downright embarrassing. She is a little thrifty, or frugal, as Dad would say, but he really means "cheap." My mother has a coupon for a coupon, and she never buys items at regular price—NEVER! I know that she saves tons of money, but who has time? Certainly not the grocery store workers. I watch friendly, welcoming cashiers transform into irritated, angry villains every time my mom pulls into their lanes. On a good day my mom has thirty to forty coupons. And on a bad day, you don't want to know just how many pieces of paper my mom can hold in her small hands. It is embarrassing with a capital E!

Her main flaw, though, is her inability to let me grow up. Mom tends to be overly protective. I can't leave the house unsupervised. She has been my shadow for eleven years—and I want some sunlight! That's why Reed's sleepover is such a big deal. Please, let me explain further.

My parents—well, really my mom— promised that at eleven years old, I could go to sleepovers. She doesn't make promises a lot. Mom is more of an "I'll see what I can do" kind of parent. And even though she promised, I'm worried that Mom might change her mind about sleepovers.

"It's too hot; you have bronchitis," she might say, or, "It's too cold; you have bronchitis." Now, as I recall, our pediatrician never said I had bronchitis. Mom probably got her diagnosis from the internet doctor. Don't get me wrong, I have a great mom, but when she wants to say no, she can rattle off excuse after excuse after excuse—but she promised.

Yep, she actually said the words, "I promise." Still, I'm not sure. You see, promises can be tricky, especially in my house. And now that I think about it, my mom is very clever, even a bit sneaky.

I should have checked to see if she crossed her fingers when she made the sleepover promise. My mom is a teacher, and they are exceptionally smart—at least that's what I hear her say all of the time. And while I'm not the smartest kid in the world, I can figure out some things for myself. And right now, I'm thinking that my mom tricked me when she made that promise.

You see, for some adults, a promise can be more *like a maybe.* Other grownups simply propose a *"let me see what I can do"* sort of promise. But every kid knows what a promise truly means. It means for sure, absolutely, no turning back—to infinity!

I've made promises before, and I'm sure you've made real promises too. You know, like the commitments and promises we make at First Holy Communion, Reconciliation, and Confirmation.

Well, Mom's sleepover promise was not like any of those promises. Oh, no! My mom's promise was unusual. "Shaky" would be a more accurate description. As a matter of fact, I don't believe that Mom even looked me in the eye when she made the sleepover promise. She rolled her eyes, chewed gum, took curly things out of her hair, sipped green tea, swept the kitchen, and washed the dishes—all at the same time!

Sounds pretty bogus, huh? But I'm eleven, and I've got an invitation to Reed Conti's sleepover. But most important, Mom promised.

And a promise is a promise ... right?

CHAPTER 3

DUDLEY SPARKS

V J, come and eat!" Andrew shouts. "We made your birthday breakfast: pancakes with whipped cream, bacon, and raspberry lemonade," he brags.

"Here I come, Drew."

I wipe the smoke residue from my glasses and stuff the invitation deeper into my pocket. I give the rest of the mail to Mom.

"Thanks," I say, grabbing a fork and the warm maple syrup at the same time.

"This looks delicious!"

Drew snaps, "You're welcome, but wait for Dad," he huffs.

I sit at the table and sniff the butter and whipped cream running down the sides of the slightly charred flapjacks.

"Oh yeah," Andrew continues, "And wait for Justin too." Mom stops cooking and walks over to Andrew's chair.

"Remember, Andrew," Mom says, "Justin won't be home until Thanksgiving break."

Andrew sighs. "I forgot." He tucks his head in his shirt. Mom reaches down and raises Andrew's chin close to hers.

"Thanksgiving," she says, "will be here before you can say 'Santa Claus'!" "OK!" Drew cheered. "I can't wait!" He chants, "Justin, Justin, Justin! And even better: turkey, stuffing, and pepperoni pizza!"

Mom laughs, tosses the really burnt food in the garbage, and then puts the rest on the table.

"Come on, Dad," I yell. "What are you doing? I'm hungry!" I grumble, stealing a piece of bacon from Andrew's plate.

"Hey, birthday boy, hold your horses. I'm on my way!" Dad's heavy feet clump down the stairs.

"Dad," Andrew says innocently, "we don't have any horses, do we?"

"No, Andrew." Dad chuckles. "'Hold your horses' is another way to ask your brother to be patient."

Mom stops sipping on her sugarless green tea. "Hold your horses' is an idiom. Idioms," she continues, "are groups of words that have special meanings and help us use words in a fun way."

"Oh, I get it now" Drew says, "If we don't have horses, we surely must have pizza."

"Any pizza?" Andrew asks.

Dad looks up from his plate.

"Sorry I can't stay for the family celebration," he says, "but I've got two very important meetings today."

"That's all right," I murmur, trying not to appear disappointed. A surge of sadness slumps on my shoulders. I am already upset because my big brother, Justin, can't come home from college for my birthday. Now this!

"Well, VJ," Dad continues, trying to cheer me up, "you're

finally eleven. How does it feel?"

"It feels great, Dad!"

"So what!" Andrew interrupts, waving his hand full of whipped cream.

"I'm almost five!" he teases.

Mom notices that Andrew is doing more talking and playing rather than eating his breakfast.

"You've got five minutes to finish your breakfast, young man, or I'm cleaning the table."

"Hooray!" Andrew cheers quietly.

"The food is not good," he whispers.

Andrew is an extremely picky eater. He craves three types of food: sausage, pepperoni, and cheese pizza! If you want him to eat something else, it must be hidden under thick pizza crust. My little brother can eat pizza for breakfast, lunch, and dinner if Mom lets him.

"Please eat, Andrew," she begs. Still Andrew sits. Mom arches her left eye and puts down her fork. She scowls at Andrew.

"Oh Mom," Andrew sneers, rotating and zigzagging his arms like a crossing guard, "hold your horses; I'll eat already!"

Dad and I laugh and eat at the same time. Mom mixes a wrinkly forehead, and a mini frown with her laugh. Her bubbly big eyes meet Drew's face paced eyeballs. "Eat…now," she says firmly.

The morning turned into night very quickly. My birthday celebration was great with a capital G! We watched movies, ate lots of strawberry-banana cake, opened presents, and played video games. Justin sent me two books and a pair of green and black high-top gym shoes. I opened a huge box from Dad, Mom, and Andrew. I am now the owner of a professional tennis racquet and a crisp fifty-dollar bill! And while I had an awesome day, my thoughts keep going back to Reed's party and Mom's sleepover promise.

By bedtime, I am exhausted. I helped clean the kitchen, bathroom, and family room. My head hits the pillow like a hammer smashes a nail. Before long, I hear Mom's tiny steps drag toward our room. Andrew quickly tucks his video game under his pillow so Mom won't confiscate it. She looks happy but tired. Her eyes are droopy, and her ponytail is smashed in the middle of her head. She still smells like strawberries, bananas, and coconuts.

"Who gets the first squash?" Mom utters cheerfully. "Squash" is another name for hug—because it's tighter than a hug. You sort of feel like your chest is caving in. But squashes are the BEST! Andrew always gets squashes first at bedtime. Not tonight. I lay my head safely next to Mom's heart. And boy, oh boy, is it a long squash. My chest jolts. I gasp for oxygen!

"Thanks, Mom. I had a great birthday."

I choke.

"You're welcome, VJ," she utters using her *I'm so glad that you are my son voice.*

Andrew gets his squashes, too.

"I'm turning in," Mom quietly says. "It's really late. Exhausted is my middle name," Mom adds.

"No it's not. It's Maria," Andrew utters, giggling from under the comforter.

Mom moves toward the superhero light switch near the bedroom door.

"I'm turning out the lights now," Mom announces.

"Not all of the lights," Andrew protests, popping his head from under the comforter.

"Drew, use your brain!" I suggest in a cantankerous manner.

"Just turn on your night light!"

After nine o'clock, I get grouchy.

Andrew snickers. "Oh yeah, I forgot about my night light."

"Vince," Mom says as she walks toward the door, "thanks for helping me around the house."

"You're welcome, Mom; anything for you," I say graciously. I hear Andrew giggle.

"Salami! Salami! Aw, baloney!" he yelps.

Mom bends down and gives Drew a *"you'd better cut it out"* face.

"Did you say your prayers?" Mom asks. Andrew and I both answer yes.

"Pray again!" Mom orders. She is eyeballing Drew.

"Well," Mom utters, slightly higher than a whisper, "good night. I'm pooped."

"Good night, my favorite mom," Andrew says, so tired that he can barely talk. Within minutes Andrew is still.

From the top bunk, my eyes track the bottom of Mom's pink slippers. She yawns and walks slowly out of the room.

Wait, don't go yet, I utter under my breath. Now is the time to ask about the party! Here goes!

"Mom," I say in a nervous tone, "could you come here for a second?"

I hear the echo of her tiny feet approach the room again.

"May I go to Reed Conti's sleepover?"

I utter.

Mom is silent for a second. I hate silence. After a few more seconds pass, she asks hesitantly, "When is it?"

"In two weeks," I respond quickly, trying not to give her too much time to think. Slowly, I pull the invitation from my pajama pocket, then hand it to her.

"No wonder you cleaned up," Andrew squeaks from the bottom bunk. "Quiet, Andrew; go to sleep!" I yelp, covering my head with my pillow. Mom walks over to my desk. She seems to be checking the dates on my red-and-black Chicago Bulls wall calendar. I think that she is hoping we already have something planned—but I already checked. There is nothing on the schedule that entire weekend. I wait…and wait. My heartbeat is louder than drums in a high school marching band.

I can tell that this is not easy for my mom. I don't believe that I have ever been away from her eyesight for more than a couple of hours. As my super exhausted mother searches for an answer or excuse, I wonder if she even remembers the sleepover promise.

Finally, after several seconds of deliberation, Mom responds, "We'll see." And with that, the pitter of her hushed feet and the smell of strawberries, bananas, and coconut follow her as she quietly exits. My mind goes blank. Panic stretches from one end of my bedroom wall to the next—because of two simple words: *we'll see*. And one of the words, I complain quietly, is only a contraction! All of the cleaning—not to mention me putting up with Andrew's loud mouth—and for what?

In the midst of my frustration, I realize one thing: I am beat. My eyes feel like three-pound weights. They open and close between my worry and exhaustion. The dim night rays peep between the blinds and dance above my forehead.

"Drew," I whisper. No answer. He is out.

My half-closed eyes fix on the light in my parents' bedroom. Like clockwork, if I'm still awake, I hear Mom pull her mystery box from the bottom drawer. The box is a mystery because I'm not sure what's in it or what she does once she opens the box. I think Mom prays the rosary. I am almost certain that she stores a rosary, white gloves, and earrings in the mystery box. Once Mom told me that she still has the gloves, dress, and earrings that she wore for her First Holy Communion. Mom also told me that her grandfather gave her a special rosary after her Confirmation. So every night for about ten minutes, Mom is busy in her mystery box.

Like clockwork, Andrew has a ritual at night too. Most nights, he rushes through his prayers so he can play his hand-held video game, which he hides under his oversized alien pillow. And right before bedtime, he fills his pajama pockets with grape licorice, chewing gum, or leftover pizza.

Dad usually prays early in the morning. He sits near the window facing the walking trail and the Metra train station. Nothing moves when my dad prays. Everything and I do mean everything is still. Even his squeaky leather chair is at peace. Dad saves his nights for sports, sports, and more sports! He likes to stay up late and eat chewy candy that is terrible for his teeth, according to the American Dental Association. But Dad's favorite late night snack is movie-theater popcorn with extra butter! When I can't sleep, I hear Dad chomping, chewing, and cheering long into the night. The vent near my bed is like a one-way walkie-talkie. Like now, for instance: I can hear everything!

Oh no—BOOM, CRASH, SPLAT! That is the familiar sound of movie theater popcorn with extra butter spilling all over Mom's new, brown carpet. Yeah, he's clumsy too. While Dad scrambles to clean the new, brown carpet, I force myself to rest.

Even though Mom hasn't given me permission to go to Reed's sleepover, I still feel lucky. Reed invited eight people to his party, and I am one of them.

My swollen eyes and weary spirit explode with sheer happiness. Things couldn't get any better. Ten minutes into my peaceful rest, however, I have a thought: a scary, miserable, keep-you-up-all-night kind of thought! It punches me upside my head and in the nose—TWICE! The Eighth Invitation...

Who gets the Eighth Invitation? My body shoots up and back down like a yoyo. "Dudley Sparks!" I shriek like a pathetic, whimpering wimp. My blissful thoughts of fun and adventure are obliterated and transformed into the beginnings of a restless slumber—a nightmare!

"Oh no," I screech in a miniature voice, trying desperately not to disturb the pint-sized monster who sleeps beneath me. I hear the spring in Andrew's mattress pop. Too late—the monster is awakened!

"Quiet," Andrew scowls. "Auh, shut up and go back to sleep. I've had it up to here with you," I screech, almost knocking down the ceiling fan trying to pillow pop the tiny tyrant who sleeps in the bottom bunk. "Go back to sleep!" I screech for a second time.

From the full-length mirror, directly across from our bunk beds, I observe the full wrath of Andrew's dissatisfaction with me. For a second, he is as quiet as a mosquito on skin. All of a sudden, Drew pops his head up and slaps an ugly, *you woke-me-up frown* on his face. At the same time, he searches desperately for Benny the Bull before realizing that in his eagerness to rest, he threw his stuffed bull and his hand-held video game on the floor.

My little brother dislikes a couple of things: loud noises, tags on the back of clothes, puzzles, and alarm clocks. He is a bear in the morning if he doesn't get at least nine hours of rest. In the mirror, I watch Andrew gather his pillow, game, and Benny the Bull. He perches his small body in a ball, and within seconds Andrew is out again. I try to rest. My eyes are sealed shut.

My mind races, but it isn't going anywhere. "How could I forget about the most despicable kid in school? How?" I mumble.

As the hours of darkness creep slowly by, my thoughts focus on the sleepover. I really want to go to Reed's party. "Anything," I mumble. "I will do anything to go to the sleepover," I shamefully admit to myself. I am frantic, thirsty for fun. But what am I going to do about Dudley Sparks…

And the Eighth Invitation!

CHAPTER 4

RULES, RULES, RULES!

B oys, come and eat," Mom shouts. "Breakfast is on the table!" My eyes open, then close like a trap door, swift and secure.

"Be right there," I mumble, taking a minute to rest on my soft, comfy pillow.

All of a sudden, Andrew's pint-sized voice ricochets in my ear. "Get him! Run! Jump! Escape!" Andrew shrieks.

"Keep it down, Drew," I grumble. "I'm exhausted." All goes silent—for a second. Then, from out of nowhere, Andrew's voice rockets.

"You'll never take me alive," he yells like a crazy man.

I can't see him, but I think that he is playing with his action figures somewhere nearby. He lowers his voice, but hushed words echo in my eardrums and bounce like a spinning boomerang in flight.

I hear that minuscule monster, but I do not see him. I pry my eyes open for the last time. Again, no Andrew.

From my bed, my aching eyes explore piles of clutter and confusion. I peek around blankets, above piles of smelly gym clothes, and under desks…but still, no Andrew.

"I know where he is! He is playing in Dad's office!" I mumble to myself. He is going to be in major trouble! A couple of weeks ago, we got in BIG, BIG trouble because someone (Drew) spilled apple juice on Dad's legal documents. Of course, we never found out who that someone was (Drew)!

So Dad made a new list of rules and taped them on the office door:

Rule #1: No talking back. Rule #2: Follow requests by parents the first time given. My eyes scan the list. OK I screech, …there are too many rules to list! How 'bout we skip down to Rule #83: No minors allowed in the office without an adult over twenty-one years old! This is the rule that Drew is breaking now!

Mom calls again, "Your breakfast is getting cold."

"OK," I answer. Andrew still doesn't.

I jump out of bed and head for the shower. While in there I trace funny faces on the steamy mirror. Hooray for Saturday! No homework and no major projects due. I only have to attend an altar server's meeting at 9:30 a.m., and then the rest of the day belongs to me. It will be a day full of video games, food, video games, and more food!

I brush my teeth—twice—dab on invisible acne medicine, and apply a large mass of Dad's invigoratingly fresh deodorant under my arms. Then, with water still dripping from my hair and stuffed in a bathrobe (that was too small a year ago), I head for the office in search of Drew. I spot him immediately.

"Get up from there," I demand. He is crouched between Dad's bookshelf and computer stand. He leaps in the air and bumps his head on the corner of the desk.

"Ouch!" he squeals, trying not to cry.

"That's what happens when you break rules. You bump your head," I say, with no concern for his injury.

"What rules?" Andrew asks sarcastically.

I breathe heavily—twice.

He doesn't wait for me to respond.

"You're not the boss of me," Andrew snaps, folding his long, scrawny arms tightly around his narrow frame.

"Vincent," Mom yells from the kitchen, "come downstairs and stop tormenting your brother!"

"But...," I grumble. "Auh, forget it. I'm hungry." I dart down the stairs. Andrew trails closely behind me, twisting, stomping, and jerking his body.

"Mom," he whines, "VJ thinks he is the boss of me!" Mom gives Andrew an "*unhappy teacher stare*" and politely says, "And you think you are the boss of me." I laugh inside as I grab a seat at the table, then a plate. Yuck! Cold food!

I put down my fork to reflect. Let's see... Mom seems to be giving me the cold shoulder, Andrew is acting like a clown, and I am mentally and physically exhausted. Yep, I can tell what kind of day this is going to be...

But at least it's Saturday!

CHAPTER 5

MEET MR. CARS

The last thing I want is to start a feud with Andrew. Older siblings never win. Justin never won, and I won't win either. Living in my house is not easy! Plus arguing with Drew would give my mom a reason to ground me. And if I am grounded, of course, I cannot go to Reed's sleepover. The answer would definitely be NO, with a capital N!

I would guess that "NO" is my mom's most overused word! I would also guess that she says the word "NO" one hundred times a day at school. She has twelve years of practice. I've seen her in action!

"No, YOU may not get water.

"No, you may not go to recess.

"No computer."

"No" today; "no" tomorrow; "no" forever! I feel sorry for those junior-high students!

Now, let's look at the word "yes."...I check my pockets...I can't find it. Neither can my mom! It's nonexistent in my mother's vocabulary. Like the dinosaur, the dodo bird, and the Mayan civilization: it's simply not there—gone!

The kitchen is quiet; so are Mom and Andrew. I can hear the last pieces of turkey bacon sizzle in the skillet. I frown at the food in front of me.

Andrew finally flops down in his chair to eat. He grimaces at me through his juice glass. Mom is in a grumpy mood too. Maybe she didn't get enough rest last night either. Dad, on the other hand, is always a ray of sunshine compared to Mom.

"Mom," I ask hesitantly, "is Dad around?"

"He's at the pet store shopping for a larger home for James. His fins are banging against the sides of the bowl," she says.

My eyes scan the clock. I can't be late for my meeting. I panic.

"Who is taking me to my altar server's meeting?" I didn't give Mom a chance to answer. "Not Dad," I complain, looking at the apple-shaped clock over the refrigerator again. Mom gives me a half smile. She looks at her watch. "If your father is not back in ten minutes, I will take you to the meeting," she says. My mother can read my mind. I have a great dad, but he is always late! Well, maybe 90 percent of the time.

I keep my eyes fixed on the apple shaped clock.

"Boy, this grape juice is delicious," I broadcast, making small talk.

Mom simply replies, "I'm glad."

Suddenly, a thunderous crash from outside almost shatters my drinking glass.

WHACK! BOOM!

CRASH!

"Oh no! Not again," Andrew bawls. "My ears! My ears!" he squeals. With that, Andrew drops to his knees and rolls his eyes to the back of his head. I keep eating. Mom doesn't seem to be surprised by his antics, or she simply doesn't care. On the other hand, I am always shocked and amazed at Andrew's ability to act like a total idiot!

Again the noise sounds.

BANG! BANG! KAPOW!

Drew looks for Mom to rescue him. No luck—she is busy cleaning, and she is in a grumpy mood.

"I can't take it anymore!" Andrew squirms.

"Andrew," Mom says in an irked tone, "it's not that loud. Finish your breakfast, please."

"OK, I'll try," Andrew whines.

A few seconds later: Bang … Bang … Kapow!

Andrew puts down his fork and jumps from the table.

"May I be excused?" he cries. "Go ahead," Mom says, waving her hand in frustration.

"I'm taking James to my room too," Andrew screeches. He wipes his sticky hands on his paisley, purple PJs; grabs his toast, James, the fish then shoots up the stairs. Poor Mom trails Andrew with a towel, catching dribbles of water from James's not-so-clean bowl. Needless to say, Andrew never comes back to the table.

The earsplitting clamor is produced by none other than our neighbor, Mr. Cars. He is our Friday the 13th—every day! Mr. Cars builds things … I guess. He collects rusted mirrors, nails, old pipes, and other rubbish. His front yard, driveway, and garage are home to tires, hubcaps, scrap metal, and whatever else he can find to stack in his front and back yards.

Sometimes, our neighbor's rubbish spills over into our backyard. When Mr. Cars is not home, Dad neatly piles his junk back in his yard.

Mr Cars's house is just plain scary, especially on Halloween night. Cutting the grass, trimming the hedges, and watering the plants are not at the top of Mr. Cars's things-to-do list. Personal hygiene is not a priority either! Mr. Cars wears the same clothes every day. He sports gray-and white-striped overalls over a dingy shirt that looks too small for Andrew. To make things worse, Mr. Cars always—and I mean always—wears dusty, brown leather boots. He looks awfully warm, especially in mid-August! And while I have never been close to Mr. Cars, his appearance shouts, "I need a bath—badly." The largest tool belt in the world is attached to Mr. Cars's overalls with a million keys clanging constantly. Fastened to the key ring is a blue, faded bandana that is attached to a giant, silver ring. The silver ring hangs all over the place, blasting commotion and chaos throughout the quiet neighborhood. Needless to say, everyone knows when Mr. Cars is around. He is a walking human wind chime. Most of the people in the neighborhood are afraid of him. I'm afraid of Mr. Cars a little, and Andrew is afraid of him a lot!

My strange neighbor has unkempt, uncut hair that is stuffed in a yellow, washed-out cap that is supposed to read "GONE FISHING." But of course, letters are missing. The G, the F, and the ING. Now, the hat reads "ONE ISH."

As far as I can remember, I don't recall Mr. Cars ever having a visitor. Birds, squirrels, stray dogs, and cats even avoid his house. I've never heard him speak or even seen him wave to anyone. Mr. Stevens really doesn't count because he has to deliver the mail.

Seconds pass…the noise stops. Mr. Cars is quiet. Mom is putting away the dishes. And since Andrew is locked in the bedroom, I figure that this is a good time to jog Mom's memory about the sleepover promise.

"This breakfast," I say, "is delicious."

Without turning around, Mom utters, "Thanks."

I can tell that she is grumpy, but do I take the hint? Nope! So then I ask nonchalantly, "I wonder what Reed's mother will serve for dinner at the sleepover?"

Mom doesn't say a word. Now I take the hint! I excuse myself from the table and head for the porch steps.

Obviously, I am not getting an answer about the sleepover today. It's almost time for my meeting anyway. I peep through the blinds—first, to see if Mr. Cars is in his yard. No sign of our unkind, unpleasant, unhappy, unfeeling, unhelpful neighbor.

A large bumblebee greets me as I find a cozy spot to wait for Dad. I shoo the bee away. I'm terrified of them! The bright sun parks above the hefty oak tree near the garage. The cool, fall breeze sings above my Loyola University cap. My mind takes a casual stroll. Yep, life is great! I've got frisky squirrels behind me, singing birds above me, and I can feel God's presence all around me. I check my watch. In fifteen minutes, I need to be at the church. An altar server's job is a very important one. I have a leadership role in the celebration of Mass. It is a tremendous honor. I feel like I am serving God and my church community. Once, I even had the opportunity to serve Mass with Bishop Paul at last year's seventh-grade Confirmation Mass. I felt so proud!

Beep! Beep! Dad's car horn interrupts my thoughts. "Dad's here," I yell. "OK, see you in an hour," Mom says. "Don't forget your seat belts," she adds. "See you when you get back!" Andrew shouts from his bedroom window. I guess he's not still mad at me.

On the way to the church, Dad and I chat about Mr. Cars. I explain how Mr. Cars's loud noises almost shattered the breakfast glasses. Dad laughs really hard when I describe how Mom trailed Andrew and James with a towel.

"Your mom doesn't want to ruin her new, brown carpet," Dad teases. We both laugh.

But I don't share my feelings about Dudley Sparks and the sleepover dilemma. So I keep those thoughts to myself. Instead, we joke about the different contraptions we could build using all of the junk from next door.

"We could build a spaceship and fly to the moon," Dad says.

CHAPTER 6

OLIVIA MOORE

No traffic. Dad and I make it to church in five minutes. "Your mom will be here to pick you up in an hour," Dad says with a quick wave.

"OK, have a good day," I say.

Once Dad is down Sullivan Drive, I plop my tired body down next to the statue of St. Lawrence O'Toole. The awesomeness of the bronze figure casts a shadow on the pink and white flowers near the church steps.

Joggers, bikers, big dogs, little dogs, and their owners trot across the newly paved walkway. Small white pebbles and leftover cement chunks dance in the warm morning breeze. I take a minute to enjoy the sunrise and to pray.

Honk, honk ... BEEP, beep! A vehicle approaches. Disorder, mayhem, and bedlam bombard the once-peaceful space. Joggers speed up, canines snarl, squirrels scramble, and rabbits hop higher. Puffs of gravel slap the tire treads of hurried bikers. There is no doubt that the Conti family has arrived—all ten of them!

Twelve if you include their dogs, Mayonnaise and Dixon Conti. Thirteen if you count Abraham, the snail. Reed sticks his head out of the van window, waving wildly.

"Hey, VJ," Reed yells, "you're here early."

"It's about time. What took you so long?" I shout back.

I can hear Mr. Conti shouting orders like a drill sergeant in the marines.

"No one out of this van but Mom and Reed!" Mr. Conti insists. "No one, and I mean no one!"

But before Mr. Conti parks, Reed leaps from the overly crowded Ford minivan with a football tucked under his arm.

"Dude," Reed yells, "catch!" My quick hands meet the tattered leather football. I feel something thick and sticky. YUCK! The ball smells like skunk, old garbage, and dirty socks. I drop the ball, straighten my spectacles, and wipe my hands on a nearby tree stump.

"Hey," one of Reed's younger sisters shouts from the minivan, "give Mayo back his ball."

Reed laughs. "No way—we're playing catch," he shouts to his sister. "Reed!" Mrs. Conti yells at the top of her lungs. "Put Mayo's ball back in the trunk!"

"But...but...," Reed mutters under his breath.

"You're in front of the church," his mom blasts, "not on the playground!"

Just so you know: Reed's mom always yells. She's not mean or anything like that; she's just really loud and really happy all of the time. Even when Mrs. Conti gets irritated with Reed—which is often—she rips into him with a smile. Mrs. Conti is one of my favorite parents, and she's really hilarious too. Reed, however, is relentless and stupid. He does not listen or follow directions well.

EXAMPLE #1: Reed is still tossing the football after his Mom told him to stop!

The younger Conti children are keeping up their share of commotion too.

The noise blasts from the van into the early-morning breeze. "Get off of my foot!" someone shouts. "Well, don't touch me!" Then, "Move over!" The demands go on and on.

Mr. Conti can barely keep everyone settled. "Sit down, Dixon! Mayo, stop biting! Give your sister her pacifier. Don't smash Abraham!" he rumbles. The van shakes with noise and clamor. The earsplitting screech and squabble go on! Mr. Conti is not as loud as Mrs. Conti, but he comes in at a close second.

A minute passes. The unruly behavior continues. And apparently no one in the car seems to be listening. Finally, Mr. Conti surrenders and calls for reinforcement.

"Mariam (that's Mrs. Conti), let's go!"

"I'm on my way," she yells back.

Just then, a louder commotion rings from the busy intersection. Billows of smoke fill the air as a rickety, old truck with "Market Day" printed in bold letters on its side wiggles and wobbles down Sullivan Drive.

"Here comes Mr. Adams," Mrs. Conti says. Mr. Adams is our PTO president. He does all kinds of things to keep our school running smoothly. He is always smiling. Everyone likes to be around him—not at all like his daughter, Mary Margaret Adams. We call her 4-1-1 because she knows information about everyone in the entire school. She is a Wikipedia, walking atlas, almanac, and encyclopedia wrapped into one.

"How is everyone this fine morning?" Mr. Adams asks, wearing his usual friendly smile.

"Just fine, Mr. Adams," Mrs. Conti replies.

"We're OK," I say. Reed is silent. I guess Reed knows what is coming next. His eyes gawk at the enormous truck labeled "Market Day" as Mr. Adams swings open the slightly rusted double doors.

"Need any extra hands?" Mrs. Conti asks.

"I can use all of the help I can get. We are a little shorthanded today," Mr. Adams answers.

"Well, today is your lucky day!" Mrs. Conti says, nodding her head and patting Reed and me on the back. "Here are two strong, young men ready to volunteer their services."

Reed's eyes almost pop out of their sockets. "There has to be one hundred boxes on that truck," he mumbles from the side of his mouth, careful not to let his mom hear his grumbling about volunteering.

"I'm on my way to run errands, but Reed and Vincent would love to help," Mrs. Conti replies, flashing a quick wink at Reed and me.

The Conti's drive away, and we get to work. Reed growls quietly as we begin unloading boxes.

At first, the boxes are as light as a feather, but after a while, my arms begin to ache.

"We will be here until tomorrow," Reed grumbles.

"Stop complaining," I say, trying to look on the bright side of a cloudy situation. "Maybe we'll get some free food." Reed shrugs his shoulders.

"I'm not hungry," he complains.

Hot dogs, frozen pies, double-chocolate-chip cookies, ice cream bars, lasagna, and cheesecake orders keep us busy. Luckily, after the fourth load, most of the altar servers and even some adults pitch in. Before we catch our breath, Father Francis signals for us to come into the church for our meeting.

"Thanks a lot, everyone. I couldn't have done it without you," Mr. Adams, says gratefully. Echoes of "You are welcome" bounce off the gigantic truck as Mr. Adams hurries to St. George, the next parish down the road.

Just then, Olivia Moore and her great-grandmother park at the front of the church. I get a funny feeling in my stomach whenever Olivia is around. Olivia is the nicest, most beautiful girl in the United States—no, in the world! To be beautiful is good but to be nice and beautiful is even better! Olivia has it all. She is polite, does all of her homework, and has cool-looking braces. She is awesome with a capital A!

"Look who's here, VJ," Reed teases.

Reed always spells O-L-I-V-I-A. Sometimes he sings, hums, and dances while he spells too. I think he knows I like Olivia, but I wouldn't dare tell Reed—he would blab to the whole school.

"Is she coming this way?" I ask anxiously.

"Is who coming?" Reed asks sarcastically.

I don't give Reed a chance to answer before I rush him with another question.

"How do I look?"

Reed studies me. "You look A-OK!" He gives me a thumbs-up.

"Great," I mumble.

"Glad I'm wearing the khakis with only one hole in the knee."

How is it, I reflect, that girls can make boys want to take more than one shower a day, brush, floss, and use extra cologne? Just a thought…. However, I find it interesting that girls don't seem to affect Reed's way of thinking, nor his appearance. He looks like he just rolled out of bed this morning and showed up. Reed's shirt is stained, and his face is covered with strawberry jam and bread crumbs. For a second, my attention focuses on the jam.

I mumble quietly, "Jam…strawberry jam…strawberries…" Oh no!

The jam splattered all over Reed's face reminds me of breakfast!

"Reed," I whisper, while keeping an eye on Olivia, who is still talking to her great-granny, "I had an onion bagel with strawberry jam for breakfast."

"OK, and…?"

Reed utters sarcastically, shrugging his shoulders.

"Bad breath—I've got bad breath! Do you have any gum or mints?" I plead desperately.

"I had some mints yesterday. Let me check," Reed says. He digs in his three pockets. I inhale…three times. My curious eyes carefully shadow Olivia, who is still near her car.

"Hurry up; hurry up!" I urge Reed.

"OK, OK," Reed huffs, "I've got something."

My gaze shifts excitedly toward Reed's front left pocket. He pauses…I pause.

"Last one," Reed says with a smile.

"This is all I've got. Take it or leave it," he announces. His clutched hand reveals an unwrapped, green object that sort of resembles a mint.

"It looks disgusting!" I gasp.

"I'll leave it—it's repulsive!"

"Fine," Reed says. "This is all I've got." Reed engages his bony shoulder in an up and-down exercise, then tosses the mint on the pavement near the flowerbed. "Reed, do me a favor." I move closer. "Smell my breath." I move closer—so close that I can see the tiny hairs in Reed's nose. Reed moves down a few steps, almost tumbling backward.

"Hey, get away from me," he screeches. I just keep moving toward his nose. When I get close enough, I puff, quickly blowing my breath in Reed's face. He wiggles his nose and scowls.

"Well," I whisper desperately, "what does it smell like?"

"Your breath smells just like a pound of red, ripe onions," Reed giggles.

I immediately begin rummaging around my own pockets for gum or mints, even though I know that there are none to be found.

"Just kidding," Reed smirks. "Your breath smells minty fresh."

Tap, tap, tap. I can hear the clacking of Olivia's shiny, black, patent-leather shoes and the bump, bump of her instrument banging against the church steps. I don't believe Reed—onions are strong!—but I have no choice. I'll just stand a few feet away from Olivia and scrunch my lips really tight. Olivia heads my way.

"Hi, Olivia," I say shyly. "Do you need any help with your instrument?"

I ask, trying to avoid standing too close.

"Of course Olivia needs help. She plays the tuba," Reed says, laughing.

From the corner of my spectacles, I see Olivia gaping at my face.

"What's wrong with your mouth?"

Olivia asks.

"Oh, nothing," I say, almost too embarrassed to speak. I reach for her instrument.

With a puzzled look on her face, Olivia answers, "I'm fine; the tuba just looks heavy… but thank you," she says politely.

"No problem, Olivia. I can carry your tuba. It's no problem," I say, using my courteous voice.

"Well," she says, hesitating and still staring at my weird-looking facial expression. "OK. Thanks, Vincent." Olivia smiles, then hands me the tuba.

I stretch my arm like a human rubber band.

Then I remember my breath. I back up—and then my balance bolts. I freeze. My body shuts down. My knees lock. My heart sinks.

Something is going terribly wrong! My feet are pretzels. Oh no...my feet...I lose my balance—totally! I feel my long, gangly legs turn to mashed potatoes. I am going down. Luckily, Olivia grabs the tuba before it hits the church steps, and—you guessed it—I start falling. Not quickly, but in s...l...o...w motion—the worst type of falling possible.

Olivia moves the heavy tuba to a safe place. Her great-grandmother dashes from the car like an Olympic sprinter, shouting, "Oh, Lord—don't drop the tuba! It's not paid for—don't drop it!" I try to help, but I can't because I...am...t...o...o...b...u...s...y... f...a...l...l...ing!

Every living being takes cover! Chirping robins, squirming squirrels, and rustling rabbits run for their lives! Daddy long legs, buzzing bees, leafcutter ants, and daring dragonflies scram!

Wood chips from the church steps bounce from my face and down my short sleeve polo. My glasses shoot from my face like a cannonball, clear across the church parking lot. I am surely at the lowest moment in my life.

Slam...smash...bam! My battered and bruised body finally comes to a screeching halt. Without looking up, I brush the leaves and gravel from my pants and shake my head to get whatever crawled into my ear out. I don't look up. It's too painful. I wish that Olivia would just go into the church for rehearsal.

Nothing—and I mean nothing—can be worse than facing Olivia. Well, until Olivia's great-grandmother says, "Sonny boy, can I help you up?"

Now, that's worse than facing Olivia!

"No need," I mumble, "but thank you. I just missed a step…," I utter—way, way under my breath.

I don't know where Reed is, but I can hear his muted cackles echo in the warm midmorning breeze.

After a few seconds of feeling sorry for myself, I decide that I am not a quitter. I must redeem myself. I cannot let Olivia remember me stretched out on the church steps with gravel and cement residue splattered on my face.

Reed finally manages to stop laughing long enough to hand me my smashed spectacles. I jump to my feet and give Olivia direct eye contact.

"Are you OK, Vincent?" Olivia asks with a concerned look on her face.

"I'm good; I'm good," I mutter, trying to gain back a shred of confidence. Again I stretch my arm and reach for the tuba. "Still need help with that instrument, Olivia?" I ask.

Olivia's great-granny frowns. "Honey, are you sure?" she asks in a very worried manner.

"I'm sure," I say to Olivia's great grandmother, with a colossal smile.

The instrument makes it to the choir stand safely! I am on time for my meeting—with a minute to spare!

CHAPTER 7

NOT A WORD...NO MATTER WHAT

Father Francis's meetings are always brief. Before you can spell "cauliflower," Reed, April, Chase, Fibbing Freddy, and I assemble on the steps, telling jokes and silly stories. We listen to the beautiful choir between April's pranks and Freddy's fibs. A few sixth graders join us in several rounds of "That's My Car!" I always end up with the junky car that makes lots of noise—sort of like the green machine! That's what we call Mom's worn out, dilapidated olive green van. It's a moving disaster on four wheels.

"Who's picking you up?" Reed asks.

"My mom," I say, rubbing one of my new sore spots. "She should be here in a minute," I moan.

The church is calm. All of the altar servers, musicians, and choir members either walked, carpooled, or rode bikes home.

It is silent. Reed stands, stretches, and sits. I just sit, too scared to stand.

"We're going to have a great time at the sleepover. I have lots of things planned." And don't worry, VJ, Reed continues, I won't let you near the steps at my house. "Don't worry VJ, I won't let you near the steps at my house.

I try to change the subject. "I'm really tired today," I mumble. Reed frowns. A concerned look fills his face. I guess best friends can tell when something is wrong.

"OK, Vince, what's going on?" Reed flops down right next to me. I lean back a bit so I can breathe my own breath instead of his. Reed has a real problem with personal space.

"Did your mom say you could come to my sleepover? YES or NO? Everyone else is coming," Reed says in an uneasy voice.

"Don't worry, Reed. I'm sure my mom will keep her promise."

"Great…great…," Reed bellows, shaking his head and looking down the street for his ride.

The leaves join the butterflies in a brisk morning dance. There is an awkward moment of silence.

"You know, Vince," Reed whispers, "I was just thinking about that 'clown'.

"Who?" I say, innocently. I already know that Reed is referring to Dudley Sparks, but I play dumb.

Reed whispers, "Dudley…Dudley Sparks,"

"That's who I thought you were talking about," I answer.

"Here's the problem, VJ; my mom ordered me to invite Dudley to the sleepover."

All of a sudden, Reed frantically stands and inspects the church and school perimeter. He surveys the entire two-block radius. He even looks in the trees and bushes! Sometimes he does silly things. When Reed is satisfied that no one can hear our conversation, he whispers, "My mom believes that I should forgive Dudley—that we all should forgive Dudley. Holding on to ill feelings and resentment, Mom says, will make me bitter and angry. 'Move forward,' she advises. 'If you keep looking back, you can't see all of the great things ahead. Your heart will close and your spirit will be sad,' she says."

I hold my head down. So does Reed. For a minute, there is silence.

"Vince," he whispers, "I had to take matters into my own hands." Reed stuffs his hand in his back pocket and plucks out a crumpled piece of paper. He keeps it close.

I panic! What is Reed up to? It can't be good; I can feel trouble. His surprises and bad decisions have gotten me into trouble before. So this time I stand and search the perimeter.

Looking in the trees and bushes doesn't seem like a silly idea after all.

My eyes take a journey combing through every possible place a person could hide. We are safe. Reed slowly tells me his plan.

"Mom thinks," Reed whispers, "that I put all of the invitations in the mail, but I didn't."

Reed holds his hand closed tight. My eyes almost pop from their sockets. This time I invade his personal space.

"You are unbelievably insane!" I stammer. "What ... wha ... are you crazy?" I yelp at full volume!

"Well ... not really crazy," Reed jokes, "but my dad says I act nutty sometimes ..."

"Stop fooling around!" I screech. "Did you forget that your mom knows Dudley's mom?"

I did not wait for an answer. "Your mom knows everyone's mom—did you forget that?"

"Nope," Reed answers, "I didn't forget. But I'll just have to take that chance."

Reed puts on a brave face, but I know better. Sweat from his thick caterpillar brows skid down his large, chubby cheeks. I see tension and stress all over his face.

The warm, unruffled breeze now seems like a chilled arctic blast. Icy saliva slowly slides past the massive lump in my throat. When I do things wrong, my teeth chatter. My neck and arms collect goose bumps. I'm scared!

Reed waves for me to move in closer.

"I've got something to show you." Reed whispers. He hands me the crumpled piece of paper. I unfold it, slowly. There it is: a grimy, grungy mess that reads:

Dudley Sparks
2507 Carpenter Ave.
Park Forest, IL 50765

"Last week," Reed whispers, "I mailed an invitation to Alex, Walker, Zander, Nelson, you, and my two cousins, Ray and Ryan. Here's the eighth one. I just couldn't drop the invitation in the mailbox," Reed whines.

"Well," I say forcefully, "I surely don't want it!"

I try to give Reed back the invitation, but something bonds my fingers to the dirty, crumpled paper.

"What is this sticky stuff?" I ask, shaking the grubby invitation loose.

"I had Belgian waffles, so that's probably syrup and butter," Reed answers. I inhale—**twice.**

"Reed, why don't you just throw it away? The mail carrier is not going to take it anyway." I hold up the pathetic piece of paper. "Look! The stamp is almost gone," I squeal in frustration.

"Throw it away? I can't throw it away!" Reed yelps. "I promised my mom that I would mail all of the invitations. I just didn't say when."

A few minutes pass. Once again, the familiar sounds of pandemonium and chaos fill the peaceful environment.

Quickly, Reed grabs the *Eighth Invitation* and stuffs it carelessly in his back pocket.

"Don't drop it," I warn Reed.

He nods and says, "I've got this— don't worry."

"Come on, Reed," Mr. Conti yells.

"We've got to take your sisters to volleyball practice, your brother to the library, and the dogs to the vet!"

"OK, I'm coming," Reed bellows.

"Vincent, need a lift?" Mrs. Conti yells from the extra loud van.

"No, thanks; I'm fine."

Reed moves closer so his family can't hear our brief conversation. I listen carefully. As my partner in crime slithers away, I stare at the *Eighth Invitation* that is tucked haphazardly in his back pocket.

I wonder if it is safe there. I wonder if one of his siblings will find the invitation and give it to Mrs. Conti.

In just that moment, I wonder about ten different things— none of them good. My eyes watch the *eighth invitation* slowly fade from my protective sight. My mind recalls our brief conversation:

"Vince, not a word—no matter what," Reed murmured.

I paused for a quick second. Then the word "OK" slowly rolled from my blithering brain to my trembling tongue.

"Not... a word...," I garbled.

"... no matter what."

CHAPTER 8

YOU'LL GET A PORSCHE...
WHEN PIGS FLY

I had a mental list of activities planned for my only day off. I actually thought about practicing for my upcoming piano recital or reading a couple of chapters from my favorite mystery series. And since I struggle in math, I probably could practice subtracting fractions with unlike denominators...

NOPE—I just found out that Dad has other plans: cleaning the garage.

Ever since I can remember, our garage has been filled to capacity with things that we rarely use, like Mom's (never-worn) ice skates, five fishing poles, camping equipment, and an unfinished swing-and-slide set that Dad never put together.

Our garage oozes over with boxes of baby clothes, old computers, unplanted tulip bulbs, encyclopedias, a file cabinet, two smashed bikes, and a lawn mower with four missing wheels. Wait!

There's more!

Rusted rakes, broken tools, and a rickety, red fire truck are placed next to Andrew's alien spaceship, which is really a refrigerator box. Christmas decorations and hundreds of other useless things give our garage a capital M for messed up!

To say the least, the garage is the pits! I should have known this day was coming. Mom says it's a miracle that we have not seriously injured ourselves entering and exiting this booby trap that we call a garage. So far, Dad twisted his ankle on a skateboard. And just two weeks ago, Andrew bruised his leg on a broken riding toy. And yesterday I jammed my fingers searching for an air pump.

So, needless to say, today is cleaning day. From the kitchen I hear Dad moving stuff around. "Andrew," Dad calls.

"Vincent," he calls even louder, "I need your help!" The voice of doom has spoken.

Mom is already in the garage…just standing there, fussing and pointing. "Move this; toss that!" she orders. "We could win first place for the sloppiest garage in the neighborhood," Mom criticizes, raising her hands in exasperation.

Of course Andrew disagrees. "Oh, no," he argues, "Mr. Cars takes first place. Have you seen that heap of jumbled junk in his garage?"

"Don't talk—just work," Dad orders. "The Bears football game starts in a couple of hours."

"This will take more than a couple of hours," I complain, eyeballing the hills of clutter and chaos. "How did it get this way?" I ask with a sigh, gawking at the untouched stacks of stuff. "I've got my own agenda, and this is my free day," I rant until I get tired, even though no one is listening. "Well, this is absolutely ridiculous!" I whine.

Andrew interjects, pointing to a dishwasher that I broke five years ago. "Is this from the 1980s or something?" he booms. "None of these things belong to me. Most of this stuff was here before I was born," he exclaims.

"Stop complaining and get busy," Mom demands.

Minutes fly by. Then an hour. Then two hours.

"That's it—I'm exhausted!" Mom grabs the hand sanitizer. She cleans her arms, feet, and hands—twice! "Yuck!" she says. "You guys can finish—this is ridiculous," she scowls. And with that, Mom walks in the house and slams the door.

I look at Dad, perplexed. "Ya know," I say, "Mom and Drew have that slamming-the-door thing really bad." We laugh.

I hear Andrew stomping and shuffling his feet.

"I'm tired too!" he complains, reaching for the hand sanitizer.

"Put it down and keep working," Dad orders. "We're going to get rid of this junk so I can make room for my dream car." Dad whispers so Mom can't hear him, but she hears him anyway. "You'll get a Porsche when pigs fly!" Mom yells from the kitchen. We laugh. Mom laughs too.

"Is that an idiom?" Andrew asks.

"I think so," Dad says, smiling. "This job is worse than unloading the boxes for Mr. Adams," I COMPLAIN.

The more Dad moves things around, the more work he finds for us. I am beat! While Dad helps Andrew lug boxes to the large garbage cans in the back, I stumble upon an enormous plastic container, neatly taped, with a sign on the front labeled:

COLLEGE STUFF

My feet cannot get to that box fast enough. I peel away the tape and tear into the huge container. My curious eyes quickly scan the merchandise. It is overflowing with weird-looking shoes and clothes from the seventies. I know the clothes are from that era because I watch old movies from Mom and Dad's DVD case. And while all of the things in the box look hideous, one piece of clothing holds my attention more than any other. I have never seen so many bright colors in one place before. I grab it from the box. "What is this?" I mumble. I think it's a shirt…

"Did my dad really wear this?" I utter under my breath. I look for my dad, but he is nowhere to be found. I hold the garment closer to the light on the garage ceiling. The material is wacky. It stretches and zigzags at the same time. My eyes skip and scamper in confusion. I hold it to the light again because I can't believe that my dad would ever wear something like this. It is foul… with a capital F!

I hear laughter. Andrew interrupts my thoughts.

"Whose gaudy shirt is that?" my meddlesome brother asks, pointing at the odd piece of clothing. Just then, Dad drops the garbage can and broom in a panic!

"Oh no, Vincent—put that back,"

Dad protests. "That shirt is valuable."

"Oh," I say sarcastically. "This is a shirt… I wasn't sure.

Dad offers a croissant grin then frowns." My eyes return to the shirt. "This is valuable?" I ask, holding the hideous piece of clothing closer to the bright light that fill the dreary dusty garage.

"Yes!" Dad answers excitedly. "Don't throw away anything in this box, all of these items are priceless—really important and valuable," he reiterates. I am even more curious now. I search the box for other priceless items. Something immediately grabs my attention. I find what appears to be a hat. I think…

"Dad," I ask sarcastically, "is this velvet, green, red, and black hat with the long rip on the side important too?"

Dad grabs his hat. "Hey, give that back," he says.

Andrew screams with laughter. Dad laughs hysterically too. Once again, my curiosity leads me back to the container labeled "college stuff."

"What's this?" I pick up something that looks like an enormous CD.

"Put that back; put that back," Dad says nervously.

"What is this?" I ask again.

"It's an album," Dad answers proudly.

"And what is an album?" Andrew ask.

"An album is an outdated version of a CD," Dad quickly answers.

"However, what I have in my hand," Dad says in a sort of wacky voice, snapping his fingers and swaying side to side, "is priceless," he brags, "worth big money— stupid money!" He hums.

"Oh no," Andrew teases, laughing hysterically, "Dad is trying to talk cool!" Andrew is so full of funny that he can barely contain himself. He loves Dad to act silly. I usually feel embarrassed—with a capital E! Andrew, however, is beyond fascinated. His eyes roll like a cylinder going downhill. His infectious smile brightens the dim, dusty garage.

"Is that thing a movie too?" Andrew asks, reaching for the album.

"No Andrew," Dad boasts, "this is my favorite Stevie Wonder album."

Andrew glues his anxious eyes to Dad's mouth. As usual, Drew is waiting for one of Dad's long-winded speeches. And trust me, Dad has a lot of them!

"You've listened to Stevie Wonder's music before, boys," Dad says, snapping his fingers and swaying side to side.

"I want to listen to Stevie Wonder," Andrew chants!

"Not today," Dad sings. "The game will be on soon. You both need to get back to work."

"Auh, man," we groan.

While we pick up trash and toss useless objects, Dad carefully puts his items back into the container. My ears wait to hear a funny story or a long speech. Instead, I catch a glimpse of Dad's happy eyes dance with pride as he remembers the good ol' days.

For a minute, Dad is silent and very serious. His pupils dance through cluttered scrapbooks and photo albums— he seems to recognize something else important and valuable! In a flash, his strong hands grip books, magazines, and lots of other gear. The clanging of track medals and other old college stuff capture Dad's undivided attention. His face quietly smiles.

I watch my dad quietly without making a sound. Who would ever think that something so simple as a shirt or a trophy could mean so much. I am perplexed with a capital P. For a few seconds we are both quiet. Then Drew drops the dust pan on the garage floor.

"Dad, I'm really tired, he whines.

"Time to finish," says in his cheerful voice. It's almost time for the Chicago Bears to demolish the Green Bay Packers." But first, Dad secures his "valuable" stuff and carefully positions the box in the same spot, way, way back in the corner of the old, dusty semi-clean garage.

By now, Andrew and I are filthy, tired, grouchy, and smelly. So with dirt on our clothes, dust on our faces, and a musty stench under our armpits, we've had more than enough.

"I'm tired," Andrew whines. We both reach for the hand sanitizer this time.

"We're almost done," Dad says "As soon as we clean the—"

Andrew and I interrupt. "Clean the what? What else is there to clean? What else?" we cry.

Dad pauses. "Well," he says, looking around the garage, "I guess we're done. My game is on."

"Hooray!" Andrew exclaims.

"Double hooray!" I interject, sounding like a frantic five-year-old.

Mom must have heard Andrew's cheers. "Pizza's ready," she shouts. Mom always orders pizza for lunch on Saturdays. Drew and I dart to the front door. We are famished!

All of a sudden we hear, CLICK, CLICK, CLICK, BANG.

"Oh no," Andrew shrieks, "it can't be!"

CLICK, CLICK, CLICK, CLACK, CLICK.

We hear the sound of keys—lots of keys. Andrew's eyes swell. He is a Philippine Tarsier!

"Close the doors! Close them tight! Mr. Cars is out tonight!" Andrew shrieks. "Come on, VJ; I'm going in."

With these words, Andrew takes off like a roadrunner chasing a rattlesnake.

All that is left of Drew is the dust from the bottom of his shoes. He dashes for the front door.

SLAM! That's the door. CLICK. That's the lock.

ZIP, ZAP, ZIP.

That's the alarm system!

But Mr. Cars is not coming to our house; he is thumping to his rusty, dusty mailbox.

"Hello, neighbor," Dad shouts from the sparkling new garage. Mr. Cars doesn't look our way. Slowly, our unfriendly neighbor unlocks his mailbox, grabs the letters, walks into his house, and closes the door.

"Dad, that guy is rude and mean. He never speaks. He doesn't like us," I complain.

"Maybe he didn't see us," Dad answers.

"For three years? Come on, Dad!"

"Yeah, Dad," Andrew yells through the tiny holes in the screen door. "He is rude—with a capital R! I'm staying in... forever!" Andrew jeers.

CHAPTER 9

NOT A GOOD
TIME TO TALK

Monday is here again. I wake up to the smell of stale bread and wet ketchup. I peek at Andrew on the bottom bunk. He is still fast asleep, holding a slice of pepperoni pizza. The other hand secures Benny the Bull.

I tiptoe out of the room and down the stairs. Today I need an answer—either yes or no!

Mom is working out in the family room. "One, kick, and two, kick, and twist, kick," she huffs.

"Good morning, Mom. You're up early," I say. She doesn't hear me. Her exercise routine continues.

"Work your abs and tighten your tummy. You can do it—you're a winner!" Mom chants with the woman on the exercise DVD.

"Good morning, Mom," I say a little louder.

"Oh hi, VJ," Mom says breathily.

"How'd you sleep?" she asks.

"Pretty good," I reply. "My face is wide awake, but my body is still trying to catch up."

Mom chuckles. Laughter and a happy mood are a good sign, I say to myself.

"I'm almost done here, Vincent. Why don't you take your shower, and I'll get breakfast on the table," Mom suggests. My stomach rumbles. "Can I eat first? I'm really hungry."

"Sure," Mom retorts, turning off her exercise DVD. "What would you like to eat, VJ?" Mom always calls me VJ when she is in a chipper mood.

"A plain bagel, three scrambled eggs with onions, Swiss cheese, and orange juice is fine....On second thought, Mom, never mind the onions." "OK, no onions," she says.

I stand next to my mom while she scrambles the eggs. I try to find the courage to ask about the sleepover. Then, from out of nowhere: "Look out, Vince! RUN, MOM—I'll protect you!"

Andrew is awake.

He comes crashing down the stairs dressed in his last year's super tight Halloween costume, yelling about creatures from outer space. "My light saber can save us. I'll protect you," he roars. Andrew shoots in front of Mom and extends his arms, waving his weapon like a Ninja seeking retribution against all wrongdoers in the galaxy.

"You're my hero," Mom exclaims, pretending to be a helpless space mom in distress. "Thank you, Andrew—you saved me," Mom cheers in a silly voice, almost scorching my scrambled eggs.

After a minute more of Andrew's antics, he swings his cape behind his back, loosens his last year's Halloween costume, and scurries up the stairs, waving his light saber and shouting, "KA-POW!"

For a second, Drew is quiet. Then, all of a sudden, a loud "Ouch—that hurts!" echoes throughout the once-quiet kitchen.

"Oops! I'm sorry, Dad," Andrew screeches!

"That's all right," I hear Dad say. I didn't see what happened, but I'm sure Dad got smacked upside his head with the light saber.

I am right. Dad staggers into the kitchen rubbing the side of his forehead. Mom laughs.

"Andrew," Dad gripes, "be careful with that thing! You're dangerous," he says, still rubbing his head.

"OK," Andrew yells from the bathroom.

"And by the way, Space Ninja" Dad yells up the stairs, "get ready for school!"

"School? What's school?" Andrew asks, chuckling loudly. "Space heroes don't go to school!" Then, KABOOM....BANG— Andrew slams the bathroom door.

Andrew is definitely Dad's favorite. I am amazed at how much my younger brother gets away with. Justin and I would not have seen daylight if we'd cracked Dad upside the head with a piece of thick plastic. We'd also have to hear a long lecture about toy safety and being too old to still have imaginary space enemies.

Mom kisses Dad on his bruised forehead.

"Did that kid have too much sugar this morning?" Dad asks.

I shake my head no. "Other than stale pizza, no, sir," I answer.

"Well," Dad says, "Mrs. Rose is in trouble today." Mrs. Rose is Andrew's teacher.

I grit my teeth, trying to ignore the ruckus that Drew is creating upstairs.

"Honey," Dad says, looking at Mom but listening to the earsplitting racket busting through the bathroom door, "remember to go over the do's and don'ts list before Drew gets out of the green machine."

"I'll remember," she sniffs, still giggling and wiping tiny tears from her rosy round cheeks.

I grab my lunch and head for the front door, muttering under my breath, "Thanks a lot, Andrew…"

Mom must have noticed my somber demeanor.

"We'll talk later; I promise, Vincent."

"Sure," I garble, barely opening my mouth.

Today was the perfect day to get permission to go to the sleepover. But unfortunately perfection exploded into a battle of aliens with extra loud sound effects, a too-tight Halloween costume, and a red, shiny bump on the side of Dad's head. I give up! There's no peace in this house!

We actually arrive at school on time, in spite of Andrew's antics and Mom's dilapidated, green van. My mom cherishes the green machine. That's what I named her van. But if she thinks that the green machine is going to last forever, she is wrong with a capital W. The electric windows stop halfway up, the windshield wipers swish to the left but not to the right, the air conditioner only works in the winter, and the heat only works in the summer. The sliding doors don't slide— they stick! And sometimes the horn actually honks.

When Dad talks about getting a new van, my mom argues, "Oh no—I'm keeping this van forever. It has sentimental value," she says. Sort of like Dad's weird clothes, I guess. But at least Dad keeps his things hidden in a corner. Mom drives that van in public.

"Mom, are we late?" Andrew asks as he quickly gathers his jacket and book bag.

"No, Andrew, you are not late; it's just 7:40," Mom says.

"Good, I want perfect attendance like VJ."

While Andrew is fiddling around searching for his school stuff, I reflect. This is a great school, I say to myself. My mind fills with the sounds of laughter and small talk. Gray pants, plaid skirts, burgundy sweaters, and white polo shirts dance in the morning sun. People driving vans, trucks, cars—large and small—are all there to drop off their lucky kids. It is total chaos and calmness at the same time.

Parents of preschoolers and kindergarteners hold a tight grip while older kids scamper, skip, and scurry back and forth. I wait patiently for Mom to recite the usual list of do's and don'ts to Andrew. Every morning she reminds him of the same things.

"Andrew," she says, "Do all of your work but don't rush. Don't be a superhero at school; be a super learner. Do not get out of your seat without permission. Do not cut your friends in line. Do not borrow snacks from anyone's lunch." Mom stops talking for a minute.

"Finally," I whisper, "she's done!" Nope—she is just resting her throat.

"And last, Andrew," Mom pleads, "do not wear your glasses at recess if you're playing soccer."

"OK, Mom, I will…AUH…no, I won't…Auh, I'm confused!" Andrew shrieks.

My ears listen, but my mind is working. And I am thinking that by the time I get to eighth grade, it will take Andrew an hour to get through his list of things to do and not do.

After our morning prayer, I jerk the sliding door several times. It finally creeps open. I walk briskly. After a second I search for Andrew and wave to Mom."Hold your brother's hand and watch for cars! Be great," she says.

CHAPTER 10

WALKER THE MAGNIFICIENT

I let go of Andrew's hand as soon as Mom drives out of the school lot. He is too big to be holding my hand. Today, of all days, I want to be left alone. But not less than a minute after Mom leaves Sullivan Drive, the taunts of the bullies, John M. and Nick Z., ring in my ears.

"Hey, tree," Nick shouts. I keep walking.

"You hear me, skyscraper?" John cackles. John and Nick are losers with a capital L. They have detention regularly and spend time with the principal every Friday for bullying.

"Andrew, ignore them." I barely get the words "ignore them," off my tongue before Andrew turns and charges toward John and Nick. "I'm going to…" Andrew stammers.

His body is rigid. He is a bear. His eyes narrow. His face pops. "Nobody and I mean nobody talks about VJ but me and my big brother Justin." "Well," he adds in a huff, "maybe my parents and his friends can, but not you!" he screams in frustration. The bullies chuckle.

"Oh yeah, and my grandma! And that's it!" Nick and John roar with laughter. Once again, the tyrants pollute the air with contemptuous words that stick to my chest like Andrew's space bullets. Yes, words do hurt!

"You hear me talking to you, Too Tall Jones

"Keep walking, Drew," I say in a calm voice. I snatch his sweaty hand and carry him like a sack of potatoes toward the school entrance.

This is nothing new. John and Nick have always teased me about something. Usually it is my shoe size or the green machine. However, my acne outbreak is the most recent topic of their unending mockery.

Again, they jeer. "Wimp, chicken, bumpy face!"

My feet can't move fast enough. Andrew is fighting me every step of the way. I can almost read the tiny print under the *Blue Ribbon School* banner near the "Welcome to Saint Lawrence O'Toole" sign. I almost make it to the front door.

Then my eyes search Drew's. Tiny tears form a straight path down his favorite yellow-striped shirt. I've had enough! I turn to confront the bullies.

At that moment I hear a crashing RUMBLE SCREECH CRASH! The sizzling sound of a skateboard storms through the bustling parking lot.

"It's Walker the Magnificent!"

Andrew shouts.

"Good morning, idiots," Walker yells, gawking at John and Nick. They try to ignore Walker, but Walker is unrelenting.

He dodges, darts, and dashes super close to John and Nick

without touching them. Nick's beady eyes tighten. John's lips quiver with fear.

"If you run over my feet with that skateboard, I'm going to tell," Nick yells. He is so furious at Walker that he can't control himself.

"I, I... will go straight to the principal and tell!" Nick threatens.

Walker laughs really, really loud. "Need a ride?" Walker asks sarcastically. "I will personally escort you; hop on!" he shouts.

Once again, I try to avoid trouble.

The sleepover is my main priority right now.

"Andrew, Walker, let's go!" I shout, forcefully this time.

John and Nick smirk. "Hey, Vincent," John sneers, "may I borrow your canoes— oops, I mean your shoes?"

I turn around and slowly walk up to John. I invade his personal space. My angry eyes don't blink once. Even though his breath is kicking like a kangaroo, I meet his crinkly, red eyes. I take a breather. Then I contemplate as we stand toe to toe: You don't want to fight or get suspended, and you don't want to be a poor role model for Andrew. My heart and mind tell me two different things that both make perfect sense.

I step back, leaving a space between the bully and my anger. My lips move unhurriedly. "One day," I whisper. "One day..."

The bell rings. John stands frozen like the Terracotta Soldiers in China.

"Let's go, Andrew and Walker.

They're not worth our time."

"Yeah, they're not worth our time," Nick repeats in a silly voice.

"Think of your own words, you...you...fake student!" Andrew yells.

At that moment, Walker shouts, "WATCH OUT—a collision!"

And with that, he rams into the two villains. CRASH, slam, crash! They fall to the ground—hard!

"You're chopped liver!" John and Nick shout. "You haven't heard the last from us," they threaten. Then Nick quickly gathers his supplies and heads for the front door. The upset bullies groan maliciously, grind their teeth, and pound their fists, "You'll pay—you'll pay for this!" they bellow.

All of a sudden, John's book bag explodes and splits in two. Glue sticks, gel pens, erasers, markers, notebook paper, and sticky notes fly everywhere.

"Cool!" Andrew shouts.

We stand and watch school supplies rain all over the parking lot and playground.

"Sorry, guys," Walker yells. "I didn't mean to make you drop your supplies and incomplete assignments. I would help you, but the second bell is going to ring in a minute."

Can you spell "flabbergasted"? You could knock John and Nick over with a feather. The two tyrants pick up their scattered belongings—again—and mumble a few words about telling Mrs. Do-Wright.

"Wait till I get my hands on you!" Nick shouts.

Walker the Magnificent takes off as fast as his skateboard can carry him. The second bell sounds, just in time.

My watchful eyes stay fixed on John and Nick.

"Walker," I whisper, "I sure hope they don't go to the office."

"Let them go—who cares?" Walker says, waving his hand and doing a fancy skateboard trick at the same time.

We head toward the entrance door.

Mrs. Rose greets us.

"Good morning," she squeaks in her inch-high voice. Even

though we can barely hear her, we all say good morning.

"Time to line up now, Andrew,"

Mrs. Rose says.

"See you later, alligator," Andrew giggles.

"After a while, crocodile," I add.

He swings his imaginary light saber and waves good-bye. I wave good-bye too. Then I walk faster to catch up with Walker.

"I'll trade ya," Magnificent says. "You take my twin sisters and box turtle; I'll take Andrew."

"No way," I reply. We both laugh.

Walker and I laugh a lot.

The tick, tick of Walker's shoestrings click against the freshly waxed floors as we walk toward Unit B. Walker's loud feet are like Mr. Cars's clanging keys: People always know when Magnificent is around.

Mr. Frasier, the playground supervisor, lunch monitor, guest teacher, library assistant, and office clerk, approaches Magnificent and me. He has Dudley with him—and Dudley is not happy.

"Tie those shoes, Walker. You're ruining these nicely waxed floors," Mr. Frasier barks impatiently—as usual.

"Oh, yeah, sorry." Walker reaches down to tie his laces. Dudley just stands there with his hands in his pants pockets. He doesn't speak, and I don't speak to him. Our eyes never meet.

After Walker ties his shoes, Mr. Frasier and Dudley head for the office. I wait. When I think the two of them are far enough away, I slowly turn around and move my eyes to what I thought would be Dudley's back. But unfortunately, I meet the whites of his cold, antagonistic eyes. I can feel his mockery and contempt. Quickly I turn away—my feet move fast.

"He seems to be able to read my mind," I mumble.

CHAPTER 11

WHAT IS THAT DISGUSTING SMELL?

We pass Unit A without getting into any more trouble. "Two minutes and counting," Alex shouts as he scurries past us to get to his locker. We just take our sweet time.

"Peee-U!" I wave my hand to block the unexpected stench that slaps me in the face.

"What is that disgusting smell?" I gasp, holding my breath and squeezing my nose at the same time.

"It's coming from Unit B," Walker howls, "and it smells like road kill," he adds.

Immediately, I panic.

"Oh no, Walker!" I shriek. "Last Wednesday, Mrs. W. asked me to clean my locker. Today is Monday, and I forgot all about it! Gotta go!"

I dash to Unit B. But before I can get to my locker, Mrs. W.

steps out of the classroom into the hall. She is not wearing her happy face either!

"Stop right there!" she says with a scowl, holding out her arms like an over zealous referee at a wrestling match. Her disapproving grimace shoots through me like a sharp arrow. I hate getting in trouble. My teeth chatter and my bones shake. I wait for her lips to move. I take a second and swallow my saliva as I search for courage and excuses.

"You've got five minutes," Mrs. W. scolds. "No," she snaps, "you have three minutes to get whatever is decomposing in that locker out of this building!"

"OK, Mrs. W," I mumble. I would lower my head in shame but I look down, but I need to see who is hanging around to witness yet another of my embarrassing situations. I stand frozen.

After a few seconds, Mrs. W. moves her arm that blocks the entrance to the classroom. "Open it. Open it," she demands. pointing to my locker.

I try to speak but no words are available. I am thirsty with a capital T. I stumble over my parched tongue. Mrs. W. interrupts my inability to put a complete sentence together. "Vincent," she yelps sharply, "I don't want to hear any excuses get busy" she orders.

I move toward locker number 84. My unhappy teacher hovers over my shoulder like a red-tailed hawk hunting for prey. I lift the handle to open the locker.

"Never mind, don't open it" she interrupts. "You may come into the classroom for announcements and prayer, but immediately after announcements, get busy, cleaning this catastrophe that you call locker 84." Mrs. W. commands.

My feet drag slowly into the room. I am greeted by fifty-six curious eyeballs— fifty-eight if we include our pet hamster,

Norman. Announcements are brief. I see Mrs. W. eyeballing me as she writes "Saint Francis of Assisi" on the whiteboard.

My body can't get to my locker fast enough. Screech! I open locker number 84. The offensive odor hits me like a ton of bricks.

"How did all of this stuff get here?" I quietly complain. I rake, ransack, and rummage through my smelly locker in search of the culprits that caused all of this trouble.

First, I find an old pair of gym shoes and my lucky winter hat. Next, I uncover a week-old P&J sandwich, two stale cupcakes, moldy mandarin oranges, and a half-opened carton of chocolate milk. "This is disgusting," I mumble.

From out of nowhere, I hear Mrs. W.'s voice. "You're right about that, young man!" Mrs. W.'s quiet foam shoes and quick tread give her the ability to walk on air. She appears in one place, and before you know it, she is in another.

"I've got everything out of my locker," I garble quietly under my breath. Even though my mom taught me to always look at the person I am speaking to, I look at Mrs. W.'s super long neck instead.

"Thank you," Mrs. W. says. "Now throw away all of that rubbish and don't let this happen again! Oh yeah, empty this can outside, please," she says, adding a croissant-like smirk. It isn't a whole smile—just a half. And with that, Mrs. W. turns and walks into the classroom without making a sound.

"Sorry about that," I mumble softly to the back of her super long neck. My strict teacher ignores my apology. My eyes fall. So does a piece of my heart. I hate spoiled milk, hats with lint balls, and rotten mandarin oranges—and I hate getting in trouble even more!

CHAPTER 12

SEEING IS BELIEVING

After I haul the garbage to the outside bin, I head for the classroom. And you'll never guess what I see. An elephant! That's right. There is a colossal but gentle looking creature with large ears and a trunk resting on my desk. Its grimy feet and foul odor invade our classroom, just like my stale cupcakes and spoiled milk infested the hallways of Saint Lawrence O'Toole School. Of course, no one but me sees the elephant, and no one smells it but me—because it's a mirage! You know, an illusion: something that's not really there. My mind sees the elephant, but my eyes see a note sitting on my desk. Not just any note, but a note that reads:

TOP SECRET
about the you-know-what
and the you-know-who!

I am flabbergasted!

How can something be top secret if everyone knows the secret? Furthermore, Mrs. W. has a rule about notes. It is a simple rule: NO NOTES!

I dash to my chair and try to hide the elephant—I mean the note. As I slink and slither into my too-small chair, the elephant slowly vanishes.

I shake the rocks out of my brain. Real life sets in again. The letter is definitely from Reed. It looks just like the invitation that he pulled from his pocket Saturday—grubby, scrunched, and crumpled. I take a quick glance. Yes, the note is from Reed, of course—sloppy, silly, irresponsible, inappropriate Reed! I almost wet my pants!

Quickly, I wedge the note in my already-too-crowded, undersized desk, between overdue library books, three balled-up C-papers in math, and an open bag of sour cream and onion potato chips. Whatever is on this piece of paper will have to wait until lunch. I mumble softly, there is no way that I am reading a note during class—never, ever, ever!

The girls in our class think differently about notes. When it comes to writing and passing notes, the girls could get a PhD in noteology (this is not a real word)! They are skilled, trained, and organized note passers. They can transcribe, circulate, and pass information all day and never get caught—never, ever, ever!

Mary Margaret Adams—or 4-1-1, the number-one note passer—knows everything about everybody. She sits to the left of me and hovers over my shoulder all day. She monitors my every move. It's like she's writing my biography or something.

I bet 4-1-1 knows how many times I cough in an average day, what kind of dinner I eat on Thursdays, and what color socks I wore three weeks ago. She knows more about me than…me.

Tap, tap, tap. The sound of the white board helps me refocus. While Mrs. W. writes notes for the religion quiz on the board, I search my desk for my favorite erasable, black pen. Suddenly, the note from Reed ricochets from my desk and lands two feet from 4-1-1's black shiny new loafers. I quickly snatch the note and shove it back into my super crowded desk.

"What you got there?" Mary Margaret howls suspiciously. A slow chill runs up my spine. She sounds exactly like the big, bad wolf in "The Three Little Pigs." I don't open my mouth. Again, 4-1-1 sprays meanness everywhere.

"What you got there?" she drawls, using a despicable face to intimidate me. I smirk, shrug my shoulders, and play dumb.

"Got where?" I answer, grabbing my erasable pen from my desk. "This?" I say, pointing to the pen. What did I do that for? Now 4-1-1 is fuming, frenzied, and furious all at once!

"No, not that, clown," Mary Margaret growls. "I'm not a fool. It looks like a note from Reed," she rants. "A secret note…about you know who…"

My eyes pop! "We all know that Reed's penmanship looks the same as it did in kindergarten," Mean Mary snarls, I can't get a word in. She is relentless!

Suddenly, I hear Mrs. W. call my name.

"Vincent?"

"Huh?"

Quickly, I correct myself. "Yes, Mrs. W?"

"What can you tell me about Saint Francis of Assisi?" she asks.

4-1-1 clears her throat.

"Uh. Um." I struggle to find words. I clear my throat too, stalling for time.

Mrs. W. waits patiently for me to share information about Saint Francis, ignoring all of the eager hands waving in the air.

"Saint…Francis. Saint…Francis," I say, quickly as I scan through my incomplete religion notes

"I'm ready," I say confidently, using my smart voice. "Saint Francis of Assisi is known as the Patron Saint of animals, birds, and the environment." All heads turn toward me.

I continue. "Every year, we have a ceremony honoring animals around his feast day on October 4."

"Excellent, Vincent. Anything else?"

"Let me think." I flip through my notes again. "That's all I've got," I mumble. I need to take better notes, I say to myself. "Wait…um…um," I say, stalling. Mrs W. waits, looking at me…, looking…, looking…, still looking…

It seems like our hamster, Norman, is even waiting.

Finally, Lewis raises his hand.

RING!

"It's time to switch classes. You can go first tomorrow, Lewis," Mrs. W. says.

CHAPTER 13

THE HOLLOW TREE

L unchtime!
I can't get to the hollow tree fast enough. My brain is fried! I am worried about the note that Reed left on my desk this morning. On second thought, I am more than worried, I am absolutely, positively flabbergasted! While I wait for the rest of the guys to show up, I prop my tired feet on the large boulder, and munch on a bag of carrot sticks. Perched in a small burrow beside me, three local squirrels wiggle their shaggy tails and lick their razor sharp choppers, anticipating my leftovers. By the time I finish my carrots and two P&J sandwiches, I realize that I forgot my juice box in my locker.

The recess door flings open. Kids run to the playground and picnic table. Nelson and Walker detour, joining in a game of soccer with some fourth graders, while Zander and Reed butt in on a game of double Dutch.

"Get lost," the sixth-grade girls shout.

"Make me," Zander says, unraveling his feet and arms from the tangled rope. "That's what you get," Margo Jung shouts.

"Hurry up," I yell across the field. "We only have fifteen minutes!"

"No, we've got seventeen minutes and three seconds," Alex says, walking and eating at the same time. Slowly everyone finally makes it to the hollow tree.

"What took you all so long?" I complain, moving my jaws from left to right.

"Mrs. Do-Wright had us take some cans and boxes to the basement for the Saint Vincent de Paul food pantry," Alex says, wiping the sweat from his face.

"Then we moved the tables for PADS, and those tables are heavy!" Nelson adds.

"Oh," I say with a nod, still adjusting my jaws. Walker gives me a strange look. "Vincent," he says, "what are you doing with your mouth?"

"I need something to drink. My tongue keeps getting stuck to the top of my mouth. It's the peanut butter my mom buys at the store where you bag your own food. I hate that store!"

"Me too," Reed adds. "Too much extra work."

"Yeah," Zander says. "By the time I finish bagging groceries, I'm not hungry."

"You've got to buy your own bags too," Alex says.

"Anyone got an extra juice?" I blast. "I'm losing the wrestling match against my teeth and tongue."

"Nope," they all say simultaneously. Everyone is eating except Nelson. It takes him a while. He carries his lunch and schoolbooks in an old, brown briefcase.

"I'm famished, starving, and in great need of a nutritious meal," Nelson complains.

"Dude, why don't you carry a lunch bag like everyone else?" Zander chuckles. "I'm not like everyone else, that's why," Nelson replies. "We are all unique and different," he continues. "That's what makes us special."

"Forget about what Nelson carries. He can carry his lunch in a big, yellow purse if he wants to," I shriek.

"Well," Walker mumbles, "I'm all for being different, unique, and special, but if Nelson carries his lunch in a big, yellow purse, I'm speaking up!"

We laugh hysterically, but my thoughts quickly return to the note.

"Reed," I say calmly, "what about the so-called top-secret note? What did it say? And why did you just throw it on my desk?"

Of course, as usual Reed just sits there, dumbfounded.

Zander takes a minute from his delicious-looking sandwich with mayo dripping off the sides to put his two cents in. "Yeah, why?" he chomps.

Reed ignores Zander's two cents. Finally, after a quick bite from his lunch, Reed gasps deeply and shrugs his shoulders.

"VJ," Reed complains, "you need to clean your desk," he says. "I tried to put the note near the front of your desk, but everything—including the note—kept falling out," Reed grumbles.

"So you just threw it on top of my desk for everyone to see?" I shout in disbelief, waving my arms in exasperation and frustration. "You should have just read the letter in front of the entire class," I state sarcastically.

"No, I've got a better idea," Walker says, looking at Reed. "Next time let 4-1-1 deliver the note to VJ. She won't read it."

Everyone laughs. The merriment is so loud that Mrs. Coleman, the first-grade teacher, closes her classroom window. "Everybody's got jokes. Ha, ha, ha," I say, mimicking their laughter.

"Sorry, Vincent," Reed mumbles, wiping the milk mustache from his face. "I didn't think anyone would pay attention to a small piece of paper," Reed continues somberly.

"Shush. Quiet," Alex whispers. "Here comes Mr. Frasier."

"He is bad news with a capital B," Zander mumbles.

"Just pretend you're cleaning around the tree; maybe he won't come over," I mumble under my breath.

"Yeah, hurry," Nelson says, propping his briefcase against the large boulder. He still hasn't opened the briefcase yet.

We scramble through the grassland in search of paper, plastic, and cans while Reed and Walker tie their shoelaces— again.

"Good afternoon, gentlemen," Mr. Frasier yells from across the playground, using his military voice.

"Good afternoon," we say simultaneously.

Mr. Frasier walks over to the hollow tree. "Are you enjoying your lunch?" he asks. We quickly nod yes.

"Hey!" Mr. Frazier exclaims, pointing in a frantic way. "Nice briefcase," he declares.

"Thanks," Nelson retorts.

"Finish your lunch, gentlemen and thank you for keeping the grounds clean." With that, he walks away.

"What's his problem?" Nelson asks, not really expecting an answer. He continues to turn the combination on his briefcase.

"Don't worry about Mr. Frasier's problem. We have got our own," I reply, still concerned about the contents of the note.

I follow Mr. Frasier from the corner of my spectacles. When he trudges toward the recess door, Reed quickly scans the perimeter. His suspicious body language and the slow nodding of his head remind me of the incident on the church steps the other day.

"The note—the note already!" Magnificent, Nelson and Zander scowl.

Read grimaces. "OK, OK," he moans. Then Reed slowly digs deep in his beige faded khaki pants pockets and holds something tight in his always sticky hands. "The note on VJ's desk had fifteen short words on it." Reed pauses, swallows hard then slowly opens his hand. Quickly Reed passes the note to Zander.

"I always make copies," Reed brags. Zander reads it aloud:

Top secret.... I am not inviting
Dudley to my birthday party.
Is it right? Circle Yes or No

Alex takes a break from his mozzarella cheese stick, "That's eighteen words," he says.

To say the least, I am flabbergasted! I stare at Reed's forehead. "The lights are on," I say, "but nobody's home. You don't think, Reed!" I utter in a more composed manner.

Nelson looks up from his briefcase, still tussling with the lock. "But I thought your mom said you had to invite Dudley," he says quickly, trying to get back to his briefcase.

Reed stands up again and scans the perimeter around the hollow tree.

"No other breathing beings are anywhere in sight. Not even the squirrels, so sit down," I say, somewhat frustrated with Reed's idiotic behavior.

Just like before, Reed slowly pulls that same dusty and even grimier invitation from his front pocket and waves it from left to right. My eyes pop; my stomach drops, my teeth chatter and my bones ache. My bloodshot eyes follow Reed's beady eyes as he moves closer. We huddle like the Chicago Bears football team without the equipment. "I absolutely, positively don't want Dudley at my party," he whimpers, shaking his head like a stubborn three year-old. "I don't care what my parents say. I'll lie," Reed protests, still looking behind his back. His eyes search ours, waiting for a response. We focus on the frayed, crumpled, two-week-old envelope.

"He will spoil everything!" Reed exclaims. We all nod yes. No one speaks.

After a minute or two, Nelson breaks the long stretch of silence.

"Whew... finally got it," he mutters.

Nelson attacks his lunch. "What's really so bad about Dudley?" he asks, devouring his salami, avocado, and cheese sandwich.

"How much time do you have?"

Zander asks.

"I can answer that: you've got four minutes, thirteen seconds," Alex reports. "Just enough time to tell you in detail what's so bad about Dudley Sparks?" Zander adds, sarcastically. "All right, guys, close your eyes." Zander hums and wails, like we're being hypnotized. He spreads his long, thin arms inch by inch as he tilts his narrow body like wings on a jumbo jet in flight. "Let's take a journey back to...," Zander pauses, "first grade. You may remember first grade, when Dudley painted Mrs. Casper's guinea pig, Zorro, pink, wasn't it?"

"Yeah," I interrupt, "and it was a male too!" Nelson laughs out loud, sending a piece of his salami sandwich flying into the sandbox.

"Yeah," Reed chuckles, "Dudley told Mrs. Do-Wright that Zorro would look better pink."

"That poor rodent was never the same," Reed adds, shaking his head from left to right.

"Yep, I remember," Alex adds. "It looked sickly and walked sideways for a long time."

The fall breeze blows quietly, and the tales of Dudley Sparks continue. Zander uses his hypnotic voice again.

"Let's move forward to third grade: Mrs. Powell's class. You remember third grade? Remember the field trip to the circus?" Zander asks.

We all slowly nod yes.

"What did Dudley do when he was supposed to be going for popcorn?" Zander doesn't wait for an answer.

"I'll tell you what that clown did," Zander replies. "He switched the signs on the public bathrooms. You wouldn't believe how much trouble that caused. Boys were embarrassed, girls cried, and the adults were livid! Can you believe that?" Zander adds, frowning like he just swallowed an extra sour lemon.

Nelson tries to get a word in. He raises his hand.

"Oh no, Nelson— Wait, put your hand down. Give us a minute; we're just getting started," Reed says.

"Let's see... Dudley swallowed a key at Olivia's party, so instead of eating cake and ice cream, we all ended up in the emergency room until our parents picked us up!" Walker huffs.

"And then there was the time," Alex says, "when Dudley glued all of our gym shoes together before the fourth-grade basketball championship game."

Walker chimes in. "Then there was the time that Dudley filled all of the sugar bowls with salt in the lunchroom!" I finally get a turn to speak.

"Remember when Dudley put goldfish in all of the toilets in the girls' bathrooms. Can you spell 'catastrophic'? Most of the girls went home or used the boys' bathrooms—all day!"

"So, Nelson," Reed says, acting like a Supreme Court Judge, "now do you understand why I don't want Dudley to come to the sleepover?" Our eyes search Nelson's countenance, not necessarily for an answer but for affirmation. All is silent The wind swirls. Trees dance. Wood chips pop and semi damp soil lay low. All is silent again.

Nelson sits as still as the tiny, red ants feasting on the left over peanut butter and jelly sandwich I dropped near the playground.

"Somebody say something!" Reed demands.

"Well, I'll say something!" I utter, almost too embarrased to speak. "I'm afraid to sleep in the same room with Dudley." "Me too," they all say simultaneously.

"Take a vote," Reed says. "Thumbs up, Dudley's invited. Thumbs-down, he gets a fake invitation after the party and I blame the mail carrier for not delivering it on time." Reed adds. I think of Mr. Stevens.

Still, in spite of everything I was taught I give a thumbs up. We all did. Reed slowly shreds the crumpled envelope into tiny pieces of nothingness. Parts of the *Eighth Invitation* shoot over the bronze statue of Saint Lawrence O'Toole, across the large crucifix near the church, and around the preschool playground. The gentle wind captures our underhanded secret and distributes the tiny bits of evidence far, far down the road and way past Sullivan Drive.

CHAPTER 14

ALLERGY SEASON AND BED HEAD

I t is allergy season! I wheeze and sneeze. Andrew boohoos, sniffs, and snorts. I probably got three hours of sleep last night. To make things worse, I keep worrying about something, … but what? The alarm clock sounds. I hit the snooze button and stuff my head under my pillow.

"Time to get up, boys, or you'll be late," Mom says as she flicks on the lamp next to my bed. Drew is numb. "I heard lots of sneezing last night; it's time for you boys to take your allergy medicine."

Andrew peeks from under his comforter.

"Mom," he whines, "did you know that on any given day, ten thousand American children miss school because of allergies?"

"I didn't know that, Andrew," Mom answers.

"You're a teacher; you should know that kind of stuff," Drew complains.

"Get out of bed, Andrew. You too, Vincent," she commands. "I'll be back in five minutes," Mom adds.

Andrew mumbles something and turns over. I don't want trouble, so I yank myself out of the bed.

"Ouch!" I trip over Andrew's army tank. "Drew, wake up!" I reach over and give him a gentle nudge—or as gentle as I can under the circumstances. My foot really hurts.

"Get some of these toys off the floor," I yell. Seconds pass. He doesn't budge. I jolt his lanky, limp body again.

"Pick your things up off the floor!" I demand.

"Leave me alone; I'm tired," Andrew mumbles.

"You're tired," I say sharply.

"Tired is my middle name!"

"You kept Benny the Bull and me up all night with your sneezing," Andrew complains.

I pause for a minute, then I grab Andrew's stuffed bull right from under his pint-sized body. I whack and wallop the innocent bag of cotton and foam. "See, Andrew," I say. "It doesn't hurt!" I shriek. "Ya know why? It's made of cotton! It can't feel tired. It can't get sleepy, sick, angry, or anything else! It doesn't have lungs or any real organs. It can't breathe, man. It's not real. It's a toy!

"The real Benny the Bull is on the court," I yell, pointing to my Chicago Bulls poster.

"Shut up, Vincent! Benny is real, and he plays basketball like me!" Andrew protests.

"Well, let's just see what this bundle of cotton can really do," I say mockingly. With a quickness, I send Andrew's best buddy flying over my basketball hoop. It bounces from the rim and lands on top of an old slice of pizza, face down.

"See: Benny the Bull didn't feel a thing." I sneer.

Andrew grabs his bull, wipes the tomato sauce off his horns, scoops him under his paisley PJs, and hops back into bed. "You clean the room yourself," Andrew retorts. To say the least, I am livid. "Dad," I shout, looking for reinforcement, "Andrew won't pick up his toys!" No answer.

So here I am, with a junky room, a fractured foot, now a sore throat from all of the yelling, and a mom who still hasn't given me permission to go to my first sleepover.

I've had it! I call louder this time, to the strict, controlling, bossy parent. "Mom! Mom!" I yelp, sounding like Mr. Conti. "Andrew is going to make me late for school."

No answer.

My rant continues, "I can't find my uniform and book bag under all of his junk!"

She doesn't answer, but Dad finally does.

"OK, I'll be right there," he says.

Andrew peeps from under his comforter.

"Dad can deal with you!" I threaten. I grab my towel, toothbrush, and my too tight robe and head to the shower.

From the bathroom, I can hear Andrew putting up a fight to stay in bed.

"No, no; I'm tired. I'm exhausted. I'm sick—really sick!" he shouts. His whining continues. "Give me Benny, Dad. Give me Benny the Bull!"

It's going to be one of those days, I say to myself. A quick shower is what I need to energize me and clear my mind space. The warm shower and hazy mist clear my sinuses. I feel a little better. I tie my dark-blue, tattered robe and apply my invisible acne tonic all over my face. And of course I brush—twice.

Clouds of steam from the warm shower fill the hazy bathroom and rest on the ceiling. I scribble:

Andrew is a spolied br...

on the bathroom mirror when I am interrupted by the sound of the doorbell. Ding-dong. Who is at the door at 7:15 a.m.? I complain to myself.

"Get the door, Vincent," Mom yells from downstairs. I sigh. "I'm not dressed yet," she adds.

"Great," I mumble as I pull my too tight house robe a bit tighter, grab my foggy spectacles, and head to the door. "Yes, who is it?" I sneak a quick look through the peephole, but I don't open the door. Are my eyes playing tricks on me? Do I need thicker glasses? Or am I awake in my own nightmare? It's Mr. Cars! Mr. Cars!

In all of the years that he has lived next door, Mr. Cars has never come to our house. He is scary—double scary. Triple scary! I have never seen him close up before. I feel like I am in a horror movie. All I need now is for scary music to play in the background, the lights to go off, and my family members to disappear.

It's Friday the 13th all over again!

Mr. Cars knows I am behind the door. He can hear my stuffy nose and see my bulging eyeball. He can hear me breathe...he can feel my fear. Should I open the door and greet him? He isn't a stranger, but he is strange. I don't know what to do.

"Who is it?" Mom bellows from the downstairs bathroom.

I can't talk. "It...it...it's Mr. Cars," I whisper. I search for more words—like "help," and "save me."

Seconds go by. He rings the bell again. I wait for Dad, but he is still tussling with Andrew. I take another peep.

"Oh no," I whisper to myself, "he's got something in his hand, and it looks like a weapon." I dash.

"Dad, Dad, Mr. Crazy—I mean Mr. Cars—is here," I shriek frantically.

Dad releases the choke hold he has around Drew's neck.

"Did I hear you say… Mr. Cars is at the door?"

"Yes," I whisper in a quiet voice, trying not to let Mr. Cars hear my words. Andrew overhears though! He falls into a wild frenzy.

"Let me go, Dad," Andrew cries. "I'm getting out of here!" Andrew breaks loose from Dad's grip, snatches poor James, and zips up the stairs and slams the door. BAM! Click!

I follow Dad to the door. I am so close on Dad's heels that if he stops, I will leave size-ten track marks up his back. Cautiously, Dad opens the squeaky front door.

"You OK, Dad?" I ask. He nods yes.

I take cover behind Dad and the door. Through the gaps in the wood door, I study Mr. Cars like a paleontologist studies dinosaur bones. I stretch my eyes tight, watching his every move.

"Good morning, Mr. Cars. What can I do for you this morning?" Dad asks hesitantly.

"Morning, sir," Mr. Cars says courteously.

I can hear everything from behind the door. The odd man's pitch baffles me.

He sounds nothing like I thought he would sound. His voice is cheerful, vibrant, and friendly like the greeters at Sunday Mass. Mr. Cars pauses for a minute, then says, "I was wondering, Mr. Jones, if you have a hammer I could borrow. Mine seems to be broken."

"Sure," Dad says.

Then, out of nowhere, Mr. Cars raises his hand where the weapon rests. Oh no, I think to myself, Dad's a goner. I wedge my eyelids together.

Waiting… nothing. I open my closed left eye. And what do I see? A large, metal sign. It's just a sign! I am relieved!

Mr. Cars shows Dad the sign.

"I want to put this sign in the front yard," Mr. Cars says.

Dad nods. "I think that I can help you, neighbor," Dad says kindly. He stretches his long neck behind the door and asks me to search in the basement for the hammer.

"OK, Dad," I say. It's not a weapon at all, I mumble to myself. It's just a sign! But what a great sign it is!

MAJESTIC HOUSE FOR SALE
REAL CHEAP *CALL QUICKLY*
(718) 456-8967

In a flash I return with the hammer. "There you go, Dad," I utter, standing behind the door. Dad hands the hammer to Mr. Cars.

"Thank you, sir; I'll bring it right back," Mr. Cars says.

"Take your time," Dad replies.

Dad waves. Mr. Cars waves back. The jingle-jangle of keys signals that Mr. Cars is on the move again.

CHAPTER 15

WAIT! NOW I REMEMBER WHAT I FORGOT!

M om, Andrew, and I finally pull out of the driveway. We see Mr. Cars hammering the sign in his front yard. We make it to school on time. Mom starts the do's and don'ts list before we make it into the parking lot. I kiss my mom good-bye, even though I still don't have permission to go to the party—yet! Andrew kisses Mom too, even though he wanted to stay in bed.

I hope that Nick and John don't bother us today. And they don't! I pat Andrew on the back, give him a pound, and walk over to the fifth-grade line. I see Dudley talking to Margaret. Hummm....I wonder what those two are talking about.

Probably nothing good.

Wait—I gasp! Oh no. Wait! Now I remember what I forgot. THE NOTE!

I forgot to take the note out of my desk! I have to get into the classroom and destroy that incriminating evidence.

Walker, Reed, Nelson, and Alex walk a few feet ahead of me. When Reed stops to grab grape licorice from his lunch, I catch up with him.

"Where are you going so fast?" Reed asks. "The bell didn't ring yet," he adds, checking his watch.

"I saw Dudley talking to Mary Margaret this morning," I whisper.

"So what?" Reed says, shrugging his shoulders and chomping on the last bit of his licorice. "Who cares?" he says.

"I think 4-1-1 poked her nose in my business while I cleaned locker #84 the other day!"

Reed listens but doesn't seem concerned about the note, or anything else for that matter.

"Hopefully," I shriek, "the note is still buried under books somewhere in my desk. I have to get rid of the evidence."

I dash, leaving Reed in my dust.

Mrs. W. is standing at the door. She's smiling today.

Hurray! I cheer under my breath.

"Good morning, Vincent. You're in a hurry."

"I think I misplaced something very important," I huff, trying to catch my breath. "Excuse me, Mrs. W." With that, I dash into the room.

First, I check my messy desk. Nothing. I check again. This time I pull everything out. Still nothing. I rummage under the bookcase, near the garbage cans, and around the prayer table. Still nothing! I give up.

The last bell rings. 4-1-1 strolls past my desk and gives me a really scary smile. Then she creeps toward her locker in the hallway.

"I bet she has the note!" I say softer than a whisper. My head silently explodes with anger!

Mrs. W. interrupts my mean thoughts. "Please take out your science books," she says enthusiastically. Science is Mrs. W.'s favorite subject. I enjoy science too.

"OK, class," Mrs. W. says, "we are going to begin our unit on biomes. Who can tell me what biomes are?"

Lewis Dorsey, the smartest kid in the universe, raises his hand frantically. "Lewis," Mrs. W. says, "what can you tell us about—" But before Mrs. W. finishes her question, Lewis rattles off tons of facts about biomes that cause my head to spin—twice!

"The world has six major biomes," Lewis says. "The desert, taiga, tropical rainforest, deciduous forest, grassland, and the tundra."

While Lewis rambles on, I peep on his desk to see if he is reading from the science book. Nope—it's all in his head. Like a cornucopia of fruit, Lewis pours out important information into our unoccupied, unused brain space. He knows it all! The class quietly listens.

He continues, "Each biome has its own kind of animals, plants, soil, and climate. Let me explain further," Lewis lectures.

Alex gets fidgety. "Tick, tock—time is moving," Alex utters quietly under his breath. I laugh.

Finally, Mrs. W. interrupts. "Thank you, Lewis."

"You're welcome," Lewis says proudly. "But...I'm not finished," he murmurs. Small giggles fill the room.

"Can anyone else share something or tell about a trip you've taken to a rainforest or desert?" Mrs. W. asks, looking around the room. No hands go up, except you know who!

"I know more," Lewis exclaims, waving his hand eagerly.

"OK, Lewis," Mrs. W. says. "Thank you." Lewis goes on and

on for a few more minutes about…who knows what? Small giggles fill the classroom once again, bounce off the freshly painted walls, slide against the shiny, wooden floors, and ooze down the long, quiet hallways.

"Quiet, please," Mrs. W. says, interrupting Lewis's long, long dialogue. "Lewis" Mrs. W. says with a polite smile, "has given us an excellent overview. We have a lot of information to cover in this unit, so I'm going to make this a group project."

Oh no! A group project again! I am in trouble Mrs. with a capital T. Having a partner could be great and terrible at the same time. And while there are kids who work really hard, I'm almost scared to think about the people who could be in my group.

My eyes bounce around the classroom. Let me see…Tabitha G. could be in my group. But I hope not! She does just enough to get by. Her life's goal is to become a professional cheerleader.

According to Tabitha, cheerleaders don't have to read or study—just cheer. So, of course, I will have to do her portion of the project along with my own. Or…I could be in a group with Lewis, and I would not have to do any work at all.

Karla Vela would be OK. She's really smart, but she has a really soft voice like Mrs. Rose, so I would have to do all of the talking. My eyes search the room. Oh no—Mary Margaret! I could actually end up in a group with her. I almost forgot about 4-1-1—Ms. W.'s voice snaps me back to the task at hand.

"You will become experts on one of the six major biomes," Mrs. W. announces. In five days, you will present interesting facts about your assigned biome. Projects should include details about climate, location, plants, people, and animals. Any questions so far?" I raise my hand. "Yes, Vincent," Mrs. W. replies. All eyes are on me.

"Mrs. W.," I ask, "can we choose our groups?"

"No, Vincent, I will be assigning each one of you to a group."

I already knew that answer, but I was hoping for a different one anyway!

While Mrs. W. sits busily at her desk, I cram for my religion test. I get interrupted.

"Dudley," Mrs. W. says, looking over her oval-shaped spectacles, "didn't you go to the Swiss Alps last year?"

"Yes, I did. It was awesome—my mom and I had a great time!" he responds in a bragging sort of way.

I moan to myself. Please do not put me in his group. Please do not put me in Dudley's group. I don't like the Alps, and it's too cold, and Dudley's too idiotic, unruly, and plain ol' stupid! I rant to myself.

The tropical rainforest is an easy topic. Hummm…maybe I will get chosen to report on the rainforest. I can appreciate the organic chocolate that grows under the canopy of Ecuador's rainforest and the exotic animals in the Amazon jungle. Then, too, I think the desert could be an interesting biome. I've always wanted to visit the Sonoran Desert in Arizona.

I should be studying, but here I sit worrying about who my partners will be.

Looking…looking…Hummm…let's see…

Behind me, Nelson hides his face beneath his science book. He does not want to be disturbed. It is his nap time. To my immediate left, Zander, who also should be using this time to study, is preparing ammunition for the afterschool spitball contest, while twisting his *"What would Jesus do?"* wristband.

Walker, who rarely studies, but gets straight A's, has to sit next to Mrs. W.'s reading table. Mrs. W. says she has to "keep an eye" on Walker. But maybe she needs to keep both eyes on him because

Walker brings two sandwiches—one for class and the other for lunch. He coughs loud four times so the sandwich wrap can't be heard by the teachers. Walker serves detention at least once a week for breaking rules. Two weeks ago he got caught eating hot chips during detention. Can you spell insubordination?

Then there's Alex, who sits the closest to me. Alex doesn't bother taking a book out at all. He marvels at the antique clock near the prayer table and the recycled clock on the north wall. To say the least, Alex is a daydreamer!

Reed gets his desk moved a lot. Today he is in the front near Norman. Reed sits quietly, reading comic books and finishing late assignments from other classes. Hidden under the comic books is a zip lock bag of chocolate chip cookies.

Sometimes Reed feeds Norman.

I snicker to myself because my friend's actions, choices, and behavior ooze with mediocrity. It is clear as crystal that we have lots to learn. But in twenty years, these average guys could develop a pill to cure Alzheimer. My friends and I could travel the world fighting against injustice and poverty. Or we could create a prescription to end world hunger, terrorism, and violence. I could imagine us becoming world-famous philanthropists— giving lots of money to the needy and even flying to a distant planet to create a new world where everyone is happy.

My thoughts keep churning...

Screech! It sounds like Mrs. W. is ready. Her brown, leather chair scrapes the shiny, wood floor as she stands.

"I'm ready to assign groups," she announces, "after Reed and Walker pick up detentions for eating lunch two hours early," she demands, with a sly grin. "Thought I didn't see ya, huh? I was in fifth grade once too," she says with a giggle.

The class roars with laughter. Mrs. W. likes to joke sometimes too. Once she hands Reed and Walker detentions, Mrs W. assigns groups alphabetically.

Finally, it is my turn.

"Vincent," she says. "Your group members will give us a brief presentation on the tundra."

"OH no—what in the world is a tundra? Hot weather?

Warm…cold weather? I don't know!" I scream under my breath.

"And your partners are Kendall Dudek, Mary Margaret Adams, and Dudley Sparks," Mrs. W. announces.

You can knock me over with a feather!

CHAPTER 16

TALK ABOUT PRESSURE (T-A-P)

Y ou've got twenty minutes," Mrs. W. announces, "to begin creating an innovative presentation to share with the class. Are there any questions?" No one moves— not even Lewis.

"Great," Mrs. W. says. "If there are no questions, you can quietly sit with your group members." Mrs. W. notes the time. She is precise, like Alex. "9:45," she says.

"Get busy."

In an instant, racket and clamor explode into a flurry of intellectual activity. Chairs screech, busy feet stumble, and desks are cluttered, all in search of spirals, ink pens, highlighters, and Post-it notes. I take a few seconds to gather my thoughts.

T-A-P! Talk about pressure! I am a dilapidated building waiting to be bulldozed. My feet are numb, my loopy legs quiver, and my head feels lopsided. Working in a group with 4-1-1 and Dudley is going to be a challenge.

As I expect, Dudley and 4-1-1 do all—and I mean all—of the talking. I am a rollercoaster! Dudley's words loop in one ear and out the other. I'm not quite sure what Mary Margaret contributes! After her fourth throat clearing, I tune her completely out.

On the other hand, Kendall Dudek is an asset to the group. She takes notes and volunteers to do extra research. I just sit like a bronze statue living in my own nightmare. Pigeons could perch on my head, and I would not move an inch. Lunch can't get here fast enough. And I still can't find that note! I sluggishly walk over to the hollow tree, but I have no appetite. I clear away the dried leaves and relax on the boulder near the squeaky squirrels and buzzing bees. Home sweet home, I say to myself.

It's funny how my allergies never bother me under the hollow tree. I don't sneeze or feel sick. I feel safe when I am under the hollow tree. As you can tell, it is my favorite place in the world! By the time I force one peanut-butter sandwich down my throat, Walker, Reed, Nelson, Zander, and Alex make their way to the hollow tree. This time, I don't forget my juice! "Too bad you're in the group with Dudley," Reed says.

"Yeah, you've got 4-1-1 and Dudley!

That is messed up!" Zander says, laughing. "Mrs. W. must still be mad about your locker," Nelson adds, closing his briefcase.

"No, Mrs. W. is a fair teacher when you follow the rules," I admit. "I'm glad I've got the rainforest," Walker brags.

"Last week I watched the History Channel about the Amazon rainforest, so I already have lots of interesting facts to use in my presentation."

"Does anyone know about the taiga biome?" Alex asks.

"Well," Nelson says, "I think the taiga has really long winters, tons of insects, and Christmas trees."

All of a sudden, Reed yells, "It's not Christmas time—it's party time! Forget about the projects," Reed blasts, waving his hand. "I hope everyone's coming to the best sleepover yet!" he bellows.

"I'll be there for sure," Walker adds, destroying the last of his sandwich. "My grandma packed my bags the same day I got the invitation in the mail. She says she wishes that I could stay a week!" Everyone screams with laughter. "Well," I say, almost embarrassed, "my mother still hasn't given me an answer yet."

"Just ask her again," Reed says, dripping strawberry soda all over his white oxford shirt.

I quickly change the subject. "And if someone finds that note before I do—"

Reed interrupts me. "Oh no—not the note again." He slaps himself on the forehead. "What are you worried about?" Reed asks.

"Getting drop-kicked by my parents!" I charge.

"Dude, I'm sorry," Reed whines. "Sorry?" I shriek nervously. "Sorry won't help me," I babble.

Walker shrugs his shoulders. "Don't worry about it."

"Yeah!" Nelson and Zander agree. "Vincent," Reed says, "you didn't do anything—I did it all."

"My parents are going to hold me responsible for my actions, not your actions!" I utter in a panic.

"Oh yeah, you're probably right," Nelson says, gawking at Reed. "Quick!" Reed gasps. "Here comes Mr. Frasier! Does he ever take any days off?" Reed complains.

"Lately Mr. Frasier has been making a ruckus about 'Going Green.' Find something green to throw away!" Zander says hurriedly.

I scramble through the grass and bushes looking for something—anything—to toss in the large recycling bins. Zander is right. Mr. Frasier glances, waves, turns, and walks away. We stuff paper in our pockets and sit back down. "He's coming back," Walker says. Again we rummage around for paper, cans, and green garbage.

"Vincent," Mr. Frasier says, looking directly into my smudged spectacles. He points. "See that tiny paper over there?" Mr. Frasier asks. I scan the perimeter…nothing.

I search again…nothing.

"See it, Vincent?" Mr. Frasier says, pointing erratically in every direction, like an agitated air traffic controller.

I guess he figures that I will see it better than any of the other kids because I wear glasses. He wears glasses too—real thick, old-fashioned glasses with tape holding the right arm in place. After seconds of struggle, I realize that there is a teeny, tiny, barely visible piece of paper fluttering on an evergreen branch near the sandbox. I reach down to pluck it from the sturdy green branch. As soon as I fix the extra small piece of paper in my hand, I swallow. Oh no! My eyes pop out of my head. The miniature paper is a smidgen of Dudley's invitation that the wind failed to carry.

"Vincent Jones," Mr. Frasier states in a stern, stiff voice, "your mother is here. Please go to your classroom."

With this, Mr. Frasier walks towards the school parking lot, shifting his arms like a royal guard at Buckingham Palace.

My mom's here? What did I do now?

My mind races.

CHAPTER 17

"VINCENT, YOUR MOM IS HERE!"

G otta go," I say.

"Why is your mom here?" the guys ask.

"Andrew's probably faking sick again. I'd better go and see."

I try to play it cool. Inside my heart is racing. My eyes scan the building as I look for my mom in Unit B. The last lunch bell rings.

"Your mom's here," says a third-grader carrying a crate of chocolate milk. Seconds later, two of Andrew's friends, Eric and Devin, shout, "VJ, your mom's here!"

"Is this the event of the year? Everyone knows everyone's business at this school," I complain to myself. When I finally make it to my classroom door, I see Mom talking to Mrs. W. I reluctantly walk over to them.

"I surprised you, huh?" Mom says with a long smile across her face. "Why are you sweating?" she asks. "Long story," I answer nervously, watching my mom from the corner of my right eye.

"Vincent," Mrs. W. says, "I was just showing your mom how neat and clean your locker looks and smells."

They both laugh. Mrs. W. probably told my mom about the locker incident. The last lunch bell rings. My mom turns back to my teacher.

"You have a great day, Mrs. Wolfeschlegelsteinhausenbergerdorff," my mom says.

"I guess you see why we call her Mrs. W!"

They both wave good-bye. Finally, the hectic halls are clear of curious students, eager learners, and just plain nosey kids.

"Vincent," Mom says, "can you walk me to the office?"

"OK," I respond suspiciously. On our way, I pass Nelson and Walker. "Hello, Mrs. Jones," they sing.

"Hi, gentlemen," my mom says, in her school teacher voice.

My mind races. That friendly smile and happy voice don't fool me. Inside I'm thinking, what is really going on? I bet I know! I grimace. My mind goes on cruise control. I grimace again! My sweet, innocent-looking mom can be lethal! She is looking for evidence to break the sleepover promise—and she needs Mrs. W. to participate in her ruse. I grimace with a suspicious left eye.

"I'm really nervous about you being here. It's not even parent-teacher conferences yet!" I exclaim.

Mom's slippery, sly words tiptoe from her tongue. "I was just checking on your grades, and you seem to be doing OK," she says proudly.

"Thanks," I respond nervously. "School is going pretty well this quarter."

Mom's giant smile lets me know that everything is fine.

"My throat is dry," I croak, returning an apprehensive smile.

"Well, let's get to a water fountain," Mom suggests.

We slowly walk to the office door and the water fountain. I drink; Mom talks.

"Mrs. Wolfeschlegelsteinhausenbergerdorff gave you an exceptional report, and I'm proud of you. So if you still want to go to Reed's party, you may."

"You mean," I jerk my tongue loose, "I can go?" I bellow!

"A promise is a promise, right?" she replies.

I give my mom one of the longest squashes ever!

CHAPTER 18

GOD, CAN YOU HEAR ME? IT'S ME, VJ!

I t's Saturday! I've got no worries and no plans. Well, maybe one: finishing my science project. I do have one worry. The hair on my neck stands up when I think about the lost note, so I try not to think. I have a couple of days to complete my part of the biome project, so this is the day to get it done. Mom is in the basement, Andrew is sound asleep, and Dad has gone to the health club. It's all about me! I grab a banana and a bowl of cereal and head for Dad's office. (I've got permission!)

The fresh smells of lavender fabric softener and laundry detergent escape from the vents in the basement.

Every Saturday, Mom washes, folds, irons, and talks on the phone—all morning. When the phone rings, 95 percent of the time, it's for her. I rarely get calls, and to be honest, I really don't like talking on the phone. Email is better. Your voice can crack, you can stutter or use bad English, and no one knows. When you talk on the phone, there are no take backs. I don't know how people functioned without computers, texting, and email in the olden days.

RING... RING...

"Vincent, telephone," Mom shouts.

"Coming," I bellow. I finish the last bite of my banana, then head toward the basement. Halfway down the stairs, I extend my arm like a human rubber band to grab the phone from my mom. And nope, I don't fall!

"Ten minutes," Mom says. "You've got a project to complete."

"It won't take that long," I say. "I'll be done in ten seconds." I hear her small feet thump slowly back down the squeaky, wooden steps.

"Hello?" I say in a matter-of-fact way, looking for another banana. There is no response, so I repeat.

"Hello... hello... ?" Still nothing. Then all of a sudden, just before my index finger hits the "off" button, a strange voice emerges, echoing with four horrendous words: "I found the note." Then CLICK.

Now I fall!

My life flashes before my eyes! "You ...you...you're a great kid," I tell myself. "You...you're better than a great kid.

You're a super great kid— almost a saint," I murmur under my breath. My heart races. But I keep talking to myself.

"OK, Vincent, you know the Ten Commandments, along with the Hail Mary, The Lord's Prayer, and the Apostles' Creed—and the Apostles' Creed is really long... really long! OK, OK ... let's think... "Homework is not a problem for you. Your religion homework is always turned in on time. OK, sometimes you copy answers from Alex, but ... but at least you get it in. What else? What else?

"You share. You are an altar server. What else can I say? You made brownies for the homeless in the third grade. Last year, you helped serve food to the poor at Thanksgiving. You didn't push 4-1-1's face in the chalkboard for laughing when you fell into a bucket of dirty water in fourth grade. Nope. You…you… just walked away, like Jesus would do…

"God, can you hear me? It's me, Vincent Lexington Jones…

"HEEELLLLP!"

CHAPTER 19

TIME TO THINK

My body collides into a table. From the basement, Mom yells, "What is that noise?" I don't answer. Unfortunately, it is just enough commotion to wake Andrew.

"Yeah, what is that noise, VJ?" Andrew grumbles, rubbing his eyes and chewing last night's bubble gum. Again, my mom's muffled voice ricochets between the basement walls and up the stairs. "VJ, she yells, "who called and what was that noise?"

I don't know how to answer the question. I can't tell Mom about the note. So the next best thing to do is to pretend that I didn't hear her. And, of course, with all of the bumping and banging from the washer and dryer, Mom's voice could easily be drowned out, RIGHT?

Once again, Mom's voice echoes. "Can anyone hear me up there?" she shouts. I don't move. From the kitchen, Andrew bellows, "I hear you, Mom, but I don't know who was on the phone."

"Did something break?" she yells again. Still I say nothing.

She obviously heard me fall.

"Do you hear Mom?" Andrew asks, holding a cold slice of pepperoni pizza in one hand and a glass of ice tea in another. I ignore him.

"Mom, I accidentally fell on the steps." That is the truth. I just fell last week, I said to myself. Before I gather my thoughts, Mom's tread ascends the ten creaky steps. Potato chips, juice boxes, granola bars, mandarin oranges, and a bunch of other lunch stuff topples from her arms "Let me help you," I say, eyeballing the sour cream and onion potato chips.

"Thanks," Mom says. "VJ, Andrew, don't eat one bag," she warns.

"OK," I nod. Andrew doesn't respond.

"Did you hear me, Andrew Jones?" Mom asks forcefully. "How about the pizza-flavored potato chips?" he begs.

"No, Andrew, the snacks are for lunch," Mom says.

"OK," Andrew mutters, hiding his slice of pizza in his favorite purple, paisley pajama pocket.

Usually I'd give Mom a hard time about locking up food, but today I want to be as quiet as possible. I don't say a word. My eyes follow the snacks as Mom piles them neatly in the cupboard. I hope she forgets about all of the questions that I didn't answer as I watch her lock the snack cupboard with her portable safety lock. "Who was on the phone?" Mom asks again! (She didn't forget.) My mother can ask fifty questions about gooey gum glued to the bottom of a chair. She is relentless with a capital R!

"It was…," I hesitate. "I don't know." I choke.

"What do you mean, you don't know?"

"Huh…?" I mutter cautiously, trying to avoid the question.

She raises her leery left eye. "Is something going on?" Mom suspiciously asks.

"Well, I…I…"

Mom interrupts my babbling and fires more questions faster than I can speak. "Are your friends playing on the phone, Vincent?"

"I…I…I'm not sure, Mom. Maybe we got disconnected or something," I add.

After four more quick questions, Mom slowly saunters past me with a "*something's-going-on*" look smeared across her face.

Mom shakes her head three times. "I'm going to finish the laundry, Vincent. Please empty the garbage in the kitchen and work on your biome project." "OK," I mumble.

"Andrew," Mom orders, "please feed James and read for thirty minutes." After Mom sprays commands like Mr. Frasier, she goes back into the basement and takes the phone with her. Andrew looks suspicious. I ignore his inquisitive face. My mind zips, zooms, and rockets.

I'm sure that Mom knows something. Andrew knows something too. But whoever was on the phone unquestionably knows everything! I tussle and toil, trying to complete my biome project, but all I can think about is that strange voice on the phone. Sitting at the computer is a waste of time. I can't concentrate. The focus on schoolwork takes a major nosedive with a capital N. It is time to put plan B into effect.

Dad always told Justin, Drew, and me to never put all of our eggs in one basket. That's an idiom too, I guess. If one thing doesn't work, always have a backup plan, Dad says.

There is just one problem: I can't put plan B into action because I don't have plan A yet! And I definitely don't have any eggs. I need time—time to think. I'll make a double-decker turkey sandwich with extra pickles, mayo and cheese.

CHAPTER 20

FOURTH PEW TO THE LEFT

It's Sunday. My eyeballs feel as if they are attached to my bottom lip. I am exhausted. On top of me worrying about the anonymous phone call, Andrew honked like a pig the entire night.

If he wasn't whining, he was complaining. If he wasn't complaining, he was crying. "I need tissue. I'm thirsty. I'm sick. I'm scared. I'm mad," he moaned all night. I probably got two good hours of sleep. Dad was either getting water, cough medicine, or tissue for Andrew—all through the night.

"Hurry, VJ and Andrew—Mass starts in an hour," Mom says.

On my way to the shower, I marvel at the hundreds of empty juice boxes and dirty tissue scattered all over the bedroom floor.

"I guess I know who is cleaning up that mess," I complain. "Me, myself, and I!" "Hurry, kids; grab a granola bar. We don't have time for breakfast. Mrs. Kelly is waiting," Mom says.

"I'm coming," Andrew moans, using his "I'm really sick" voice and walking extra, extra slow.

"Just brush your teeth, wash your face, and get in the car, Andrew," I say.

"Mom's not letting you stay home!"

As we back out of the garage, I notice our neighbor's *house for-sale sign* "I think he needs to paint and cut the grass before he tries to sell the house," Mom says.

"He's got to do a lot more than paint. That place is a disaster area!" Andrew says with a cough and a sneeze.

I turned and focused on Andrew's scruffy appearance. He looks sloppier than Mr. Cars and Reed put together.

"Wipe your nose," I demand, "It's crusty." Mom hands Andrew a tissue. The church parking lot is packed. Mrs. Kelly waits for my mom at the back of the church near the confessional. Mrs. Kelly is just like family—sort of like a great-grandma. She is the oldest member at Saint Lawrence O'Toole Church. Mrs. Kelly was a member of Saint Lawrence O'Toole before we had a gym, the Sullivan Center, and the computer lab. She might have even gone to the church before the school was built.

Since I can remember, Mrs. Kelly has helped organize every first Holy Communion ceremony, the Confirmation retreats, and the annual Christmas programs. There was never an event or special celebration without Mrs. Kelly sitting in the fourth pew to the left near the choir stand. And even though she is probably in her nineties, she genuflects better than most kids.

Mrs. Kelly has silvery, white hair and walks with a cane. She looks old and very beautiful—sort of like a guardian angel without the wings.

Mrs. Kelly's sight is jumbled, and her glasses don't seem to help much. She calls me Andrew, and she calls Andrew "poor baby" or "sweetheart." But like Andrew says, Mrs. Kelly is the best!

"Good morning, Jones family," Mrs. Kelly says, reaching for Dad's shoulder.

Her hands shake a little.

"Good morning, Mrs. Kelly. Sorry we're a little late," Mom says, grabbing her special friend's hand.

"You're not late—you're right on time," Mrs. Kelly says cheerfully. We head to the front of the church. The organ music starts just in time to drown out the noise as the Conti family tramples in the side doors.

"Good morning, everyone," Mr. Conti says in a football-stadium voice. The church usher frowns at him. His voice is perfect for Mrs. Kelly. She can hear every word.

"Good morning," we all say. Andrew giggles.

"Shush, please," the usher whispers, looking at Mr. Conti.

"Sorry, sorry," Mr. Conti whispers. The annoyed usher's eyes follow the Conti family as they make a frenzied but hushed trek to their pews. My eyes scan the church for Reed. I need to tell him about the phone call.

"Let's take a seat," Mom says.

I genuflect, kneel, and pray as soon as we get to our pew. I ask the Holy Spirit to guide me to do the right thing and to help me to be a person of courage and faith. In the middle of my prayer, Andrew taps me on the shoulder.

"Excuse me," he moans, looking in my direction. "I have to go to the bathroom and cough."

"We just got here, Andrew!"

"Didn't you cough at home or in the green machine?" He shakes his head no. "Why can't you cough right here?"

My worrisome younger brother shakes his head, no. He again shakes his head no. I sigh. Then I look at all of the people in church. I look at Drew, then sigh again.

"Father Francis hasn't made it to the altar, and you've got to go to the bathroom already!" I blast quietly.

Andrew just gives me a silly stare and points to the bathroom near the entrance of the church. Asking a lot of questions will not make Andrew take his seat. It will only prolong the inevitable. So I quietly raise the kneeler and tuck my already-cramped legs underneath the pew as best as I can to let Andrew pass. He gives me a silly grin as he passes.

Mom doesn't bother asking any questions because she knows that Andrew goes to the bathroom at least once every Sunday. With a smile, Mom uncrosses her legs, folds her jacket, rests her purse on her lap, places her offering in the book holder, and tilts her body sideways so Andrew can pass.

"Excuse me, Mrs. Kelly," Andrew says. Mrs. Kelly pats him on the back.

"Poor baby, you've got a cold," she whispers.

Andrew politely nods yes. Mrs. Kelly slowly removes her wire-rimmed glasses, puts her rosary in her purse pocket, straightens out her sweater, slides her cane under the pew, and turns her body to the left so Andrew can pass. Dad sits to the right of Andrew, so he only has to watch all of the commotion that Andrew creates.

After seconds of confusion, he makes it to the aisle and moves toward his destination. I can hear the honking, coughing, and sneezing. I imagine his runny nose dripping onto his lip as he exits the church. All he needs to do now is trip over his (always) untied laces or sing extra loud on his journey to the restroom. I am embarrassed!

Right when Father Francis begins the Homily, here comes Andrew, sniffing, shuffling, and dragging his frail body up the aisle.

Once again, Andrew taps Mrs. Kelly on her shoulder. "Excuse me, Mrs. Kelly," Andrew moans again. Mrs. Kelly pats Andrew on the back.

"Poor baby, you've got a really bad cold," she whispers.

Andrew politely nods yes. Once again, Mrs. Kelly slowly removes her wire rimmed glasses, puts her rosary in her purse pocket, straightens out her sweater, slides her cane under the pew, and turns her body to the right so Andrew can pass. "Excuse me, Mom," Andrew squeals. Mom uncrosses her legs, moves her purse and then her jacket, picks up her offering, and sits back in the pew so Andrew can pass.

"Pardon me, VJ," Andrew exhales pitifully. Once again, I tuck my already cramped legs underneath the pew as best as I can.

Finally, Andrew sits down. I lower the kneeler. This scenario goes on and on. By the time we offer each other the sign of peace, Andrew has gone to the bathroom two more times. After the third trip, he and Dad stay in the back of the church. Right after Mass, I signal for Reed, Walker, Zander, and Alex to meet me at the hollow tree. Mom, Dad, Andrew, Mrs. Kelly, and the Conti's join most of the parishioners for the pancake breakfast in the Sullivan Center. I don't have an appetite. I sit at the hollow tree alone waiting to tell the guys the bad news. I have so much bad news that I can't keep up with which bad news I need to tell!

Several minutes go by. The squirrels, ants, and birds join me, hoping that I have a peanut-butter sandwich to share.

"Sorry, guys," I shrug. "It's Sunday. You've gotta wait until tomorrow." The red ants are stubborn. They stick around. But the squirrels and birds scamper toward the giant, green garbage cans labeled "Please Don't Litter."

"Mass was great!" I say in a low voice as I take in the brisk, fresh air. For a few quiet moments, I sit in my favorite spot in the whole world—the hollow tree. I mull things over, praying for guidance and compassion. Praying helps you put things into perspective, my granny always says. But for some reason, I can't figure out how I got into this mess. A quiet rumble interrupts my peaceful surroundings. It is the thud of Walker's untied shoelaces bouncing off the soggy morning grass.

"What's so urgent?" Walker yells, running with a plastic fork in his right hand and clutching a container filled with leftover flapjacks in his left hand.

"Where's Zander, Reed, and Alex?" I frantically ask.

"They're on their way."

Walker chomps, still finishing his breakfast. I almost ask about Nelson, but he attends the Baptist church down the street.

Eventually, everyone takes a seat under the hollow tree.

Slowly, I tell the guys about the phone call. Once again, they are flabbergasted!

"The anonymous caller is probably searching for my phone number right now. I'm in big trouble," Reed announces. "Vincent, did you recognize the voice at all?" Alex asks.

"Nope," I answer, shaking my head somberly. "But…but maybe it's Mary Margaret," I mumble, choking on my words.

"On the other hand, it could be Dudley," Zander says.

"Or even Mr. Frazier," Walker adds.

"Well, either someone overheard us talking, or worse than that, someone found the note!" Alex says in a panic.

"We can't worry about the note or the anonymous phone call," Reed says hesitantly. "Help me figure out a plan to escape this catastrophe—and fast!" Reed begs.

"You're not in this alone," Walker admits. "We all played an active role in this fiasco." I interrupt Walker.

"We dug a hole so deep that it is hard to climb to the surface," I utter nervously, with a note of regret.

"Well," Reed whispers, "I think I have a plan." We move close.

After a few minutes, the sounds of shuffling feet and loud giggles emerge from the Sullivan Center. Gradually, car doors slam, engines roar, and brakes screech as busy families with full bellies— and revived spirits—exit the parking lot. And as usual, we are the last to leave. Andrew and I listen to the familiar adult chitchat as parishioners and visitors walk to their cars.

EXAMPLES OF FAMILIAR CHITCHAT:

"Wasn't Mass wonderful this morning?"
"How about that choir?"
"Did you sign up for PADS?"
"Don't forget Market Day next Saturday at 9:00!"
"Who is bringing extra food for the Saint Vincent
De Paul Pantry tomorrow?"
"Where is the volunteer list for bingo?"
"Email me with that information for the spaghetti dinner."
"Where did you get those shoes?"
"I need a car wash!"
"What time is the Bears game?"

CHAPTER 21

"I'M GONNA LOSE!"

Dad snoozes on the sofa. It's so quiet that I can hear the tiny waves in James's new bowl thump against the fake seaweed. The digital clock near my bed screams 5:32 a.m. I glance out of my window in search of the sun. I cannot believe that it is nowhere in sight. This can only mean one thing, I mumble to myself.

Winter is right around the corner.

I dread winter. It is definitely my least favorite season. Along with itchy wool hats, lost gloves, lots of tissue, and dried snot, winter brings short days and cold, long nights. I'm not sure whats worse, cold weather in Illinois, sick brothers or lots of homework. I don't have homework, although Mom says that there is never, ever, ever such a thing as "no homework." If there is a book that you haven't read, you have homework. If there's a math problem left unsolved, then you have homework, she'd say.

I could work on my biome project, but I can't seem to concentrate today. I am constantly interrupted by Mom and

123

Andrew.

"Vincent," Mom yells, "could you get more tissue for Drew, please?"

"Sure," I mumble. Between getting water, juice, tissue, and whatever else his majesty needs, I can't get a thing done. Andrew has his own assistant: me! I walk from my desk to the cupboard. We have three more boxes of tissue. I grab all three, then I drag my achy feet into my parent's bedroom for the tenth time today. Andrew is under the comforter. I hand him all three boxes.

"Here you go, Drew," I say in my nicest voice.

"Thanks," Andrew answers in his most pitiful voice.

"What are you doing, Vincent?" Mom asks.

"I'm trying to complete my project," I answer curtly.

Mom ignores my rudeness. "Andrew and I are practicing for the preschool spelling bee at our Mommy and Me class next week," she boasts. "OK, Drew, first word," Mom says. "Spell 'box.'"

A blank stare settles on Andrew's face. "Ummm, Auh.., he mumbles shly. Then, "I'm gonna lose," Andrew whines.

Mom pats Andrew on his back.

Just do your best, Drew," she says.

"Just do your best." Mom hands him a tissue.

"I will," Andrew answers proudly. As I walk back to my room, I hear Andrew attempting to spell.

"Box," he says with confidence. "B...o...k...s," he slowly spells.

"I'm sorry, Andrew, sweetheart,"Mom says patiently, "the word is 'box.' It rhymes with 'fox.'"

Again, I hear him whine, "I'm gonna lose! I'm gonna lose!"

"Yep, he'll be out in round one," I mumble.

Anyway, Andrew's problems are minor compared to mine. I must get busy. My room is silent. I hear hushed movement coming from the backyard. Now it's almost too quiet to study! I hop from the desk to the bed. Then I hop from the bed to the desk. I close my eyes and reflect on the tundra biome. I realize that I don't have lots of time to complete my portion of the presentation. I stare at Dad's laptop. I pray for help. I squeeze my eyes…I got nothing! I squash my brain. Still nothing. I slowly bang my head on the desk. Mom calls me—AGAIN. "Vincent, have you completed your science project?"

"I'm almost finished," I grumble softly.

"What's 'almost finished' mean?" she asks.

"Here we go with the questions again," I say out loud with a groan. "I've got about half of my biome project done," I answer.

"That's fine," she answers back. Seconds pass. Then Mom calls yet again. "I would like to see what you have completed before you go to bed," she demands, sounding like a teacher.

"OK," I sigh. My eyes oscillate like a fan beating off the summer heat. I sink my weary bones back at my desk. My eyes are bricks. Boy, am I tired! "Trouble sure can beat you down," I say with a groan. The words on the computer seem to get smaller and smaller. I pull back the curtains and peer out of the window to welcome night. The moon dances above the tall oak tree that Mom, Justin, and I planted when Andrew was born.

YICKS! For a minute, I think I see someone in the yard. I blink. There is someone walking near my house! I pull the curtains closed and turn off the light. I adjust my spectacles and search the yard through a tiny opening in the curtain.

At first, I can't make out who it is. I move closer to the window. I open the curtains a little more. Are my eyes playing tricks on me? I say to myself. "It's Mr. Cars!" I shriek. His keys are quiet. He looks like he is crying.

CHAPTER 22

WE ALL WAIT FOR DUDLEY'S ANSWER

W e get to school without any problems. Mom's lists of do's and don'ts is brief. She has an early staff meeting today.

"Have an awesome day. I love you.

See you at three o'clock," Mom says.

"We will, and we love you too," we say simultaneously.

"Oh yeah," Mom adds, "if I'm a little late, go to extended day." We both nod OK. After two quick kisses, the green machine bounces, shakes, and rattles down Sullivan Drive.

I spot Nelson immediately.

Unfortunately, Nick and John catch my eye too. They just point at the green machine, laugh, and walk away. We both ignore their rude, immature behavior.

"Drew, go play on the swings until the bell rings," I say politely.

"I don't feel like it. I'll hang with you," Andrew replies. He follows me all of the way to the hollow tree.

"Hi, Nelson," Andrew says.

"Hey, Andrew," Nelson replies, laying his briefcase gently on the grassy landscape.

"What is that old, banged-up thing?" Andrew asks, pointing at Nelson's briefcase.

"Andrew," I say sternly, "go play with your friends."

Nelson is a good sport and very patient with Andrew.

"It's like a backpack," Nelson answers.

"Can't you just buy a backpack?" Drew asks.

I try to hush his rudeness. "Be quiet; go play with your friends," I say.

Nelson interrupts. "You know Drew," he begins, "this briefcase is very special to me. It belonged to my great- grandfather, Nelson. He carried this to school many years ago. I carry a lot of history in this old, dusty briefcase. One day, when you're older, I'll tell you a story about my great-grandfather and this briefcase."

"Wow, is it magic?" Andrew asks, looking closely at the tattered piece of luggage.

Nelson laughs. "Sort of," he chuckles.

Andrew gently picks up Nelson's briefcase and turns it around, examining the front, bottom, sides, and back.

"This briefcase isn't that bad looking after all," Drew concedes, "is it, VJ?" He looks at me, captivated by the mysterious piece of luggage.

I nod in agreement. "You're right.

It's not that bad," I say.

"Hummm...," Andrew says, "I think I want one just like this for Christmas. Yep, just like this—all banged up with rust on the side and everything!" Andrew blasts. With that, Andrew hands the briefcase carefully to Nelson and joins Devin and Eric at the playground. As soon as Andrew gets far enough away, I immediately search the perimeter for nosey people. It is safe. I slowly whisper Reed's plan to Nelson. He frowns.

"Do you really think it will work?" Nelson asks in an uncertain tone.

"Sure, it will work!" I answer, trying to convince myself. I picture the plan in my mind. This time, I frown.

"Sounds stupid, huh?" I utter. Nelson nods yes. I laugh nervously. The second morning bell rings. Math class is a total bust! I might as well be called *eraser man* because that is all I did for forty-five minutes. These fractions are choking my confidence. Mrs. Contreras is a great teacher; I'm just not a great student in math! It's like the piano—the more you practice, the better you get! I guess I need to practice!

Things are not much better in language arts. I can't locate the independent clause in a complex sentence—forget about diagramming a sentence! But to make things worse, 4-1-1 stares at me all morning. And she sends Dudley messages with her shifty, beady eyes every time Mrs. W. turns her back. They seem to be communicating in secret.

My eyes search the classroom. Reed has a blank stare on his face. He appears awfully nervous. And he should be: our plan is seriously flawed! Like I said, it's hard to pay attention to what Mrs. W. is saying. I'm not quite sure what I am supposed to be learning today. I think Mrs. W. is reviewing the parts of a friendly letter. Or is it a business letter? A thank you letter? Oh, I don't know—I'm confused!

RING. The lunch bell sounds.

Operation Eighth Invitation is in full effect with a capital F.

Students rush out the door to their lockers. Teachers head to the lounge for coffee, donuts and low-calorie lunches.

The coast is clear! The target emerges.

"Hey, Dudley," I say timidly, "wait up. I have a question about the biome project."

Dudley looks surprised. He chuckles nervously.

"You ... have a question for me?" he asks in his usual sarcastic, uncompromising tone.

"Yeah," I mutter, trying to look friendly.

"Can't it wait until science class? I'm hungry," he grumbles.

"Well ... I ..."

Dudley interrupts my babbling. "If you think I'm doing your part of the biome project, you can forget it," he states brashly.

"OK ...," I mumble.

Quickly, without speaking, my large feet steer my body in the opposite direction—far, far away from Dudley! Just then, Reed nervously rushes over. He interrupts.

"I think," Reed interjects, "that Vincent's portion of the biome project is almost finished."

"Yeah," I argue in an annoyed tone, heading for the hollow tree. "As a matter of fact, I put the finishing touches on it last night," I add abruptly.

"Well, then, what do you want?"

Dudley shrieks.

"Nothing—forget it," I grumble. The guys stand frozen with fear. Alex interrupts the hush in the afternoon breeze.

"Twenty-three minutes till the first bell," Alex announces, nervously scanning the corridors for teachers—or even worse, Mr. Frasier. Dudley stands stiff and guarded. His slender arms dangle next to his body. His caterpillar eyebrows shoot straight up to meet his frilly hair. Attached to his oval-shaped face sit two disapproving eyes that shift from left to right.

I try to read his face. It is a blank page.

"Forget about the biome project," Walker says, passing Dudley a plastic smile.

"Wanna join us at the hollow tree?" We try not to stare. We stare anyway!

Dudley responds with his body, not words. He takes a few steps away from us, then looks around. He seems to be searching for a teacher or even Mr. Frasier. And Dudley does not like Mr Frasier. This is not a good plan, I mumble. I search Dudley's eyes. He bites his lip then taps his foot really really fast. His mean gaze steals my breath.

A sixth grader bounces a basketball three feet away, interrupting the silence. After a few more awkward seconds, Dudley's mouth moves.

"Let me get this straight," Dudley says cautiously. "You are asking me—me," pointing to himself, "to eat with you," then pointing at us, "under the magnificent, super wonderful hollow tree?" "That's right," Reed says. "Let's go!" Dudley just stares.

"Under our tree," I complain under my breath as I walk a few steps ahead of the others. Dudley watches us cautiously, but he does not move.

Alex is concerned about having enough time for lunch. He twists his wrist and checks the time. "According to my watch," he says, "we only have seventeen minutes. Let's go eat!"

We walk out to the hollow tree and hope that Dudley will follow. And he does!

I unwrap my peanut-butter sandwich and head for my

favorite spot. Dudley is the last to join us. The local squirrels and ants gather. It is their lunchtime too.

Our twelve eyes watch Dudley as he slowly walks over to the hollow tree. My heart sinks as he approaches our special spot.

"What you got for lunch, Dudley?"

Nelson asks.

"Just a juice," Dudley says, taking it out of a brown paper bag. "I don't eat much."

"Well…I do," Nelson says, fumbling with his lock. Dudley looks at Nelson's briefcase.

"Nice briefcase," Dudley says. "Thanks," Nelson says with a smile. It is silent. Dudley doesn't crack a smile. He snatches the straw wrapper from his juice box and flings it on the ground. Then he takes three big gulps from the container, letting most of the juice drip onto his pants and polo shirt. After that, I watch him crush the juice box, and I hear him pass gas—at full volume. I hold my breath. I watch the straw wrapper dance in the afternoon breeze.

I mumble, "This guy is disgusting!"

Alex glares at his watch intensely and then signals to Reed.

"So, Dudley," Reed asks, clearing his throat like 4-1-1, "did you get the invitation to my sleepover?"

At that moment, everything stops! I feel queasy. My eyes fall. My ears consume me. Everything, everywhere blasts extra loud! Teeter-totters thud and bump, balls leap like lizards, and the pop of the double Dutch rope goes clip, clop, clip, clop. The fourth-grade soccer game booms and blasts in my outer ear. The seventh grade football game roars and rumbles in my inner ear. Then…loud silence. We all wait for Dudley Sparks's answer.

All of a sudden, Dudley folds his long, slender arms snugly across his chest. His right foot thumps against the moist orange and brown leaves, sending squirrels and birds up the nearest tree.

"What invitation?" Dudley scowls, almost turning purple with anger. His face screams resentment, fear, and curiosity at the same time. Dudley clenches his fists and places his watery eyes on mine, and then he slowly rolls them toward Reed. "I didn't get any invitation," Dudley snaps. He wipes the juice from his newly stained shirt. No blinks; no words. Our eyes focus on his fist, in case we have to run, dodge, dip, or dash.

"Well," Reed says, innocently, "I sent it weeks ago." Now, Reed taps his foot. He always does that when he is not telling the truth.

"Maybe it got lost in the mail," Walker says nervously.

"Or maybe your Mom forgot to give it to you," I add.

"But I didn't get an invitation!"

Dudley protests. "I didn't get anything," he yelps, sending a baby squirrel scrambling through the tall grass. "And why would you send me an invitation anyway?" Dudley squirms.

My eyes meet Dudley's. They are two full moons filled with water. My eyes, however, are filled with shame.

"You never talk to me," Dudley argues. "You guys are not my friends!" he shouts. His moon-shaped eyes scan our tight faces. We stand still, motionless! Dudley continues, "What are you up to anyway?"

"We're not up to anything," I protest.

"We're just trying to be your friend."

"Well, I don't want to be your friend!" Dudley yells. And with that, he starts toward the building. I drop my sandwich. Dudley drops a tear.

Lunch is over!

CHAPTER 23

THE ELEPHANT RETURNS

I keep thinking about Dudley. I tossed and turned last night. My feet are heavy, and my morning smile is a croissant. I should be ecstatic. I'm not.

"Well, at least I can get back to my normal life again," I say to the person in the foggy bathroom mirror.

Surprisingly there are only five pimples on my face. This acne medicine seems to really be working. I smirk, sneer, and grin, all at the same time.

Yep! Things are really looking up.

Mr. Frasier's job as sergeant is over, at least for a week. He flew to Washington, DC, to get a medal from President Obama—or at least that's what he told us the other day during recess, right after my great biome presentation.

Mary Margaret didn't clear her throat once during my part! I'm sure our group got an A+.

After our presentation, Mrs. W. gave us a full smile as opposed to the croissant smile. Dudley surprised me. He gave an excellent presentation on plant and animal life on the tundra. I tried to congratulate him on a job well done, but he barely looked my way. He wants nothing to do with me. I guess I can't blame him.

My circumstances at home seem to be running a little smoother too. My part-time job as Andrew's personal butler officially ended yesterday. Mom said that Andrew's cold is better, which means that he can pack his own books, wipe his own nose, and feed his own fish.

Yep! Things seem to be going my way. And, speaking of things that are going my way, guess what? It's party time at Reed Conti's house! Mom hands me a bag full of party gear. And she actually spent money without coupons too. She did, however, find a *"buy one, get three"* deal for socks and new pajamas. I didn't get a new robe.

"You'll get a new robe next year for your birthday."

"Just hold it closed with your hands," Mom suggested. Remember, I told you that my mom is frugal...thrifty...OK, cheap! I am not so frugal. I like spending money. I broke my bank to buy Reed a twenty-five-dollar gift card from All Mart. Mom even stopped in Zarget to buy a video game and a couple of dead flies for Reed's snail, Abraham.

"Breakfast is on the table," Mom shouts. Then, BANG... BANG...CRASH!

It is just Mr. Cars working, I think, as I prepare for school.

"Drew," I yell, "get ready for school, or we'll be late!" All I hear is our bedroom door slam and lock. But then I hear something else. Laughter. The chuckles sound familiar—but not really.

"Ha, ha, ha, ha" boomerangs outside the front door. It isn't Mom laughing, I say to myself, because she has a girly, silly kind of laugh.

Again I hear the laughter. "HA, HA, HA, HA." The clamor rings louder. Bang, bang, crash! It comes from the front yard.

I run to the window, searching for the familiar yet strange echo of glee. I stick my head out of the door and peek around the front yard. My four eyes inspect the perimeter cautiously.

Oh no! I hear keys! Mr. Cars is somewhere close. I go back into the house. The window is safer, so I peer through the curtains. New junk is everywhere—if there is such a thing is new JUNK! The enormous for sale sign blocks my view, making it hard for me to see what is really going on. I do, however, see Dad's hammer on the porch steps.

For a minute, the clanging stops, but the laughter continues. From under the mountain of clutter and confusion, I can see shoes—my dad's shoes.

"Oh no—Dad!"

I can barely breathe! My dad is in Mr. Cars's driveway! I stand motionless, helpless, and confused. A cold chill zips up and down my arms, neck, and back. And that's when I see it! The elephant is back!

He is just as grimy and gritty as before. This time he sports dirty, striped overalls with a thousand keys dangling from his pocket, a dingy white T-shirt, muddy boots, and a hat that says: ONE ISH.

"Oh no!" I shout, running to the kitchen looking for some protection. All I can find is an oversized aluminum dustpan.

"This will have to do," I mumble. So with my weapon in hand and my courage in my stomach, I charge frantically through the front door. My long, dangly legs can barely catch up with my feet. I am a gentle but fierce jaguar. By the time the screen door slams, my two feet and the aluminum dustpan meet Dad's puzzled gaze.

"Good morning, Vincent," Dad says, smiling from ear to ear. He fixes his eyes on the oversized aluminum dustpan.

I wipe the nervous sweat from my forehead and rub my eyes. I am face to face with the elephant, and just like THAT, the massive mammoth disappears: it's Mr. Cars. I rub my eyes again. Dad interrupts my dreamy state.

"Are you and Andrew ready for school?" His smile is as wide as Lake Michigan.

"Almost," I say, using a deep, bodyguard-sounding voice. "I'm just walking around practicing for karate lessons."

"You don't take—" Dad pauses. He was going to say that I don't take karate lessons, but he doesn't want to embarrass me in front of Mr. Cars.

The courage in my stomach slides to the bottom of my feet. My eyes meet my strange neighbor. I hesitantly say, "Good morning, Mr. Eleph...I mean, Mr. Cars."

"Morning," Mr. Cars says wholeheartedly.

I hide the dustpan behind my back. "Well, I'd better get ready for school," I say bashfully, trying to avoid the uncomfortable situation.

"Vincent," Dad says, "look!" He points at a shiny, slick, supercool Porsche—parked in the middle of Mr. Car's junk.

"Awesome sports car," I reply, trying to get a better look. It is buried behind the heaps of jumbled junk. "It's pretty cool," I mutter, feeling really embarrassed about the dustpan. Mr. Cars nods proudly.

"Well," I mumble, still admiring the car, "gotta get ready for school." I turn to walk away, still trying to conceal the dustpan. "I was going to clean up a mess, but I'll do it later, after karate lessons," I mutter.

"Sure, son," Dad says with a smirk. "Tell your mom I will be in shortly."

I head for the door, but I can't help but to keep turning around. I look at Mr. Cars, then at Dad…Mr. Cars, Dad, Mr. Cars—WOW!

Five minutes later, Dad comes waltzing in the house with a smile as long as the Great Wall of China. My eyes stay fixed on his every move as I gather my books and lunch. I am still surprised about him and Mr. Cars laughing like old friends. "Surprised" is not the word. Let me see….how about "flabbergasted?"

"Andrew, it's time to go," Mom says. With his book bag on his shoulder and James holding on for dear life, Andrew creeps down the stairs.

"I saw you talking to Mr. Cars.", Andrew says with a Friday the 13th expression on his face.

"Yes," Dad says, "I was. He is a nice man—a little different, but nice," Dad adds.

"I think I'm going to faint," Drew says.

"Well, can you do it in the car? I can't be late," I say sarcastically.

Beep, beep! Mom honks.

"Let's go before we're late kids," Mom shouts from the garage. I take three bites of my toast and head for the door.

"Hey," Andrew says, yelling from the garage. "The for-sale sign is missing!"

"Oh, yeah," Dad says, "Mr. Cars decided to be our neighbor for a while longer. We're going to work on cars together."

"Aw, man! Why, why?" Andrew yelps. "I thought we were getting rid of him!"

"Be quiet, Andrew, quiet." I cover his mouth. "He might hear you!" I gasp.

Dad smiles at Andrew and says, "We'll talk this evening, but for now sit quietly and put on your seat belt."

The last bell rings as we enter the school lot. We don't have time for Andrew's do's and don'ts speech today— just a kiss and "The Lords Prayer." We rush into the building.

The morning whizzes by. During religion class, Mrs. W. gives me a short speech to read for the All Saints' Day celebration next Sunday. Dudley usually volunteers to read for All Saints' Day, but this time he doesn't. He has been really quiet since the fiasco at the hollow tree. When Dudley sees me, he rushes in another direction. I feel even more uncomfortable around him now. But at least I get to sit near the choir stand for the All Saints' Day celebration.

This means that I get to sit next to Olivia! That reminds me...I need new pants!

CHAPTER 24

"MAN, YOUR BROTHER IS TRYING TO KILL ME!"

Today is the day that I have been waiting for! I leave my backpack in the green machine and dart into the house, not giving Mr. Cars's junk a second thought. He's our neighbor, and that is that. It takes me five minutes to pack my overnight bag for the sleepover.

Well, actually, I've been packed for a week! I sit on the good sofa with the soft pillows near James's fish bowl. The feisty fish emerges from under an olive green plastic plant. I put my face close to his.

"Hi, James," I whisper. His black fins bounce left to right, spraying seaweed and blue pebbles against his new bowl. "Well, James," I say, never expecting a response, "I'm going to my first sleepover. I'll be visiting Abraham Conti. He's a snail."

James does something funny with his mouth.

"No, James, you can't eat Abraham. But I will be back before you can say... well, I guess you can't talk, huh? If you could talk you would probably say, 'Hello, VJ. Ya finally busting outta here, huh? Wish it were me. Man, your little brother is trying to kill me!" I laugh really loud, sending poor James to the other side of his bowl. "Sorry, James." I check my watch.

"Mom, are you ready? I'm going to be late," I say nervously.

"Just give me a second," Mom says.

"I'm cleaning the van."

"Mom," I yell again, "did you remember to get the gift card?"

"Oh, I left it in my desk drawer," she replies. Drew runs from Dad's office.

"I will get it for you, because I've gotta pack my bags for the sleepover too."

I am a Philippine Tarsier! I am all eyes! So is James! I can't believe that my little brother actually thinks that he is going to Reed's sleepover!

I follow Andrew into the bedroom and sit at my desk. How do I find a nice way to say, "You're not going?"

"Here it is," Andrew says. "Found it! "

Drew hands the gift card to me in a hurry. "Now," Drew says, looking around the pigsty that we call a bedroom, "I have to get my toothbrush and Benny…" He shrugs his shoulders excitedly. "Maybe I won't take Benny. Andrew searches my eyes. I don't know what to say.

I clear my throat. "Andrew," I say quickly, "sit down for a minute." "I know you really want to go to the sleepover, but… it's only for…eight of us…well, really seven."

I think about Dudley Sparks and the Eighth Invitation again.

"Well," Andrew whines, "maybe I can be the eighth kid."

I pause again. "Andrew, what about the sleepover rule?" He frowns.

I ponder. "I think it's…Rule #4 or Rule #47." I try to guess.

Andrew is silent. His eyes are as still as a carnivorous sea-sponge at the bottom of the ocean.

"And remember," I say, looking at Drew's unhappy face, "Mom and Dad would really miss you."

"They'll be fine," Andrew retorts, folding his arms tightly around his tiny chest.

"We sleep with the lights off!" I blast.

"You mean all of the lights?" Andrew asks.

"Yep! All of the lights." I continue, "No night lights either."

Andrew exhales twice. "Well," "on second thought, I would really be missed at home. Mom and Dad would worry. James would be up all night…swimming…" Andrew sighs.

"It's best that I stay home."

I nod in agreement.

"And do you know who else would miss you?" I move closer.

"Who?" my curious younger brother whispers. His eyes dance across the room waiting for an answer. I use a scary voice and yell, "Mr. Cars—Mr. Cars will miss you!"

"Yikes! Oh no! Yikes!" Andrew screeches. We both laugh, way down into our stomachs. and down pass our toes. I give my younger brother a squash.

"Ya know Drew, I almost traded you for Walker's box turtles."

"Hey, no fair!" Andrew blasts.

"But," I pause, patting him on his back, "I think I'll keep you around. But if you think that's a bad trade, Justin almost traded me for a video game and a worm when I was six!" Andrew smiles and gives me a happy hug.

Mom shouts from the driveway, "Let's go, Vincent and Drew; the van is clean."

We jump in the green machine. "This is clean?" Andrew asks with a shrug.

"Mom, I'm with Dad. We really do need a new van," I say critically.

We get to Reed's house in ten minutes. I can smell the food and hear the music a block away. Mayonnaise and Dixon meet me at the corner. Reed, Ray, Ryan, Walker, Zander, Nelson, and Alex are outside playing football.

The house is decorated with banners, balloons, streamers, and lots of other great stuff.

"Wow," Andrew shouts from the green machine, "look at all of those balloons! You're lucky, VJ!"

Mom waves to Mrs. Conti. She is dressed in a penguin hat and is carrying a large tray of pizza rolls.

She's followed by Mr. Conti, who is wearing a too-tight Notre Dame football uniform and busted high-top gym shoes from the nineteen seventies.

"Food's ready," the ex–football player shouts.

"Food—I'm just in time!" I cheer, grabbing my things from the back of the green machine.

"Follow the rules," Mom says really fast, trying not to embarrass me. "And," she adds, "if you go out, wear your seatbelt. Oh yeah, be on your best behavior, Vincent."

I give her a quick hug. "I'm fine, Mom. I'm fine."

"See you around three," she says, in an *"I can't believe you're growing up"* kind of tone.

"Hey," Andrew bellows, "forget about three oclock, we will be here around 2:30. I want some leftover pizza," he squeaks. Reed knocks on the window, waving for me to get out. He is holding that disgusting football. I jump out of the van.

"Hi, Mrs. Jones," the boys yell in excitement. Mom waves.

Andrew yells, "No fair, save me some pizza!" I grab Reed's gift bag. Zander, Alex, Nelson, Walker, Ray, and Ryan run to the car.

"Hurry up, VJ," Reed says, "I've got something… well, we've got a surprise for you." Reed looks at his watch. "I don't like your surprises, Reed Conti," I mumble nervously.

Just then, a blue Chevy pulls up behind the green machine.

"The surprise is here!" Reed yells, waving his arms frantically in the air.

"And right on time," Alex shouts. Everyone waits. It is… Dudley Sparks and his mom. They all cheer! I can't believe my eyes.

"Hi, Dudley," Reed and the guys yell, running over to greet him. Once again, I am flabbergasted. NO—how about double flabbergasted! This time, there is no elephant, no mirage—just a good feeling. I don't know who is smiling the most, Dudley or his mom.

"Let me help you with your things," Reed says, grabbing Dudley's overnight bags.

"Hi, Dudley," I say shyly. This time, Dudley doesn't look sad, angry, or scared, and he doesn't turn away.

"Hi, Vincent," Dudley says in a happy tone.

"Hey, Dudley, I meant to tell you what a great job you did on the biome project," I replied. I couldn't think of anything else to say.

"You did a great job too," Dudley answers.

"Who's hungry?" Reed shouts. Everyone follows the human penguin, the ex–football player, the two dogs, and the food trays. I watch my mom slowly drive down the bumpy cobblestone road as the weeping willow trees hug the top of the green machine. Andrew's sad eyes follow mine until the green machine is out of sight. I remember sitting in that same van years ago watching Justin go to his first sleepover. Just for a second, I miss my mom. I miss home.

CHAPTER 25

THE END

To say the least, the Reed Conti explosion was everything I expected and more. It was outrageous with a capital O! My head hit the pillow around 3:00 a.m. I had a great time with a capital G! The games, the food, and the friends were the perfect ingredients for an overwhelmingly awesome event to remember.

Late that night, after everyone falls asleep, I get a chance to talk to Reed.

"I had to tell my parents the truth, VJ," Reed says in a low voice, trying not to wake the others. "I was wrong."

"No," I quietly interrupt. "We were all wrong. I felt really bad ever since the hollow tree fiasco."

"Me too," Reed agrees somberly. "Everyone deserves a chance, right?" Reed says.

I nod in agreement.

"Too much water—I gotta go!" Reed says, squirming. "I'll be right back." Reed rushes down the hall with Mayo and Dixon lagging behind his feet. My weary eyes slowly take a rest.

Then suddenly, from the bathroom, I hear a loud screech. Reed yells something. It takes me a minute to understand what he is saying. I run to the bathroom.

"Vincent!" Reed shouts. "Who put those goldfish in the toilet?"

COMING SOON

BOOK #2: SAY GOOD-BYE TO THE HOLLOW TREE

I thought the spring of my fifth-grade year was going well. Believe it or not, Mr. Cars is like a real neighbor now. And Dudley, well... he is Dudley, but a more improved one. We have all improved.

So when the bad news spreads about the hollow tree, I am flabbergasted. To make things more complicated, we have a new algebra teacher and Andrew lost Benny the Bull on a field trip.

But to make things even worse, a new kid comes to Saint Lawrence O'Toole: Lorenzo Thomas. He is a thorn in my side, not because he is a bad guy, but because he is a great guy. Everyone likes him— especially Olivia.

BOOK #3: THE FIRE

It is a warm day. Two days of watching the paint peel from the ceiling is not going to be an easy task. No TV, no computer, no video games. TRAPPED, SHUT IN, CONFINED!

That's how I feel.

I peer through the curtains to get a taste of what life is like outside of my jail cell. I can feel the breeze between the tiny cracks in the wood. Searching for a cerebral break leads me to the natural spectacles outside my door. A skunk, a vegetable garden, minuscule mutts, manicured lawns, tulips, and the barely living oak tree near our bedroom window remind me of what I am missing. My throat tickles. I cough. I smell something. It is different. Something…like smoke. We're not grilling…

Suddenly, I hear a scream like I've never heard before: "Fire! Get out!" Mom shouts. "Fire! Get out of the house!

"Where's Andrew?" Mom shouts!

I don't know…